THANKSGIVING AND OTHER HARVEST FESTIVALS

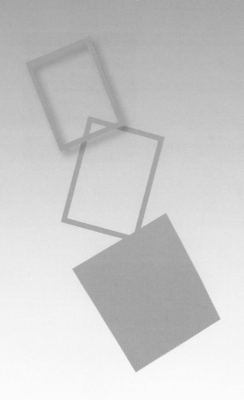

HOLIDAYS AND CELEBRATIONS

Carnival
Christmas and Hanukkah
Easter, Passover, and Other Spring Festivals
Halloween and Commemorations of the Dead
Independence Days
Lent, Yom Kippur, and Other Atonement Days
Ramadan
Religious New Year's Celebrations
Thanksgiving and Other Harvest Festivals
Western and Chinese New Year's Celebrations

THANKSGIVING AND OTHER HARVEST FESTIVALS

Ann Morrill

CHELSEA HOUSE
PUBLISHERS

An imprint of Infobase Publishing

Thanksgiving and Other Harvest Festivals

Copyright © 2009 by Infobase Publishing

All rights reserved. No part of this book may be reproduced or utilized in any form or by any means, electronic or mechanical, including photocopying, recording, or by any information storage or retrieval systems, without permission in writing from the publisher. For information contact:

Chelsea House
An imprint of Infobase Publishing
132 West 31st Street
New York NY 10001

Library of Congress Cataloging-in-Publication Data

Morrill, Ann.
Thanksgiving and other harvest festivals / Ann Morrill.
    p. cm.—(Holidays and celebrations)
Includes bibliographical references and index.
ISBN 978-1-60413-096-6
1. Harvest festivals—Juvenile literature. I. Title. II. Series.
GT4380.M67 2009
394.264—dc22

2009006914

Chelsea House books are available at special discounts when purchased in bulk quantities for businesses, associations, institutions, or sales promotions. Please call our Special Sales Department in New York at (212) 967-8800 or (800) 322-8755.

You can find Chelsea House on the World Wide Web at
http://www.chelseahouse.com

Produced by Print Matters, Inc.
Text design by A Good Thing, Inc.
Cover design by Alicia Post

Printed in China

CP PMI 10 9 8 7 6 5 4 3 2 1

This book is printed on acid-free paper.

All links and Web addresses were checked and verified to be correct at the time of publication. Because of the dynamic nature of the Web, some addresses and links may have changed since publication and may no longer be valid.

Contents

ᘒᘓ

Introduction to Holidays and Celebrations

Holidays mark time. They occupy a space outside of ordinary events and give shape and meaning to our everyday existence. They also remind us of the passage of time as we reflect on Christmases, Passovers, or Ramadans past. Throughout human history, nations and peoples have marked their calendars with special days to celebrate, commemorate, and memorialize. We set aside times to reflect on the past and future, to rest and renew physically and spiritually, and to simply have fun.

In English we call these extraordinary moments "holidays," a contraction of the term "holy day." Sometimes holidays are truly holy days—the Sabbath, Easter, or Eid al-Fitr, for example—but they can also be nonreligious occasions that serve political purposes, address the social needs of communities and individuals, or focus on regional customs and games.

This series explores the meanings and celebrations of holidays across religions and cultures around the world. It groups the holidays into volumes according to theme (such as *Lent, Yom Kippur, and Other Atonement Days*; *Thanksgiving and Other Harvest Festivals*; *Independence Days*; *Easter, Passover, and Other Spring Festivals*; *Western and Chinese New Year's Celebrations*; *Religious New Year's Celebrations*; *Carnival*; *Ramadan*, and *Halloween and Commemorations of the Dead*) or by their common human experience due to their closeness on the calendar (such as *Christmas and Hanukkah*). Each volume is divided into two sections—the first introduces readers to the origins, history, and common practices associated with the holidays; and the second section takes the reader on a worldwide tour that shows the regional variations and distinctive celebrations within specific countries. The reader will learn how these holidays started, what they mean to the people who celebrate them, and how different cultures celebrate them.

These volumes have an international focus, and thus readers will be able to learn about diversity both at home and throughout the world. We can learn a great deal about a people or nation by the holidays they celebrate. We can also learn from holidays how cultures and religions have interacted and mingled over time. We see in celebrations not just the past through tradition, but the principles and traits that people embrace and value today.

The Chelsea House Holidays and Celebrations series surveys this rich and varied festive terrain. Its 10 volumes show the distinct ways that people all over the world infuse ordinary life with meaning, purpose, or joy. The series cannot be all-inclusive or the last word on so vast a subject, but it offers a vital first step for those eager to learn more about the diverse, fascinating, and vibrant cultures of the world, through the festivities that give expression, order, and meaning to their lives.

A few of the 1,000 volunteers at Glide Memorial United Methodist Church in San Francisco work together to serve 7,000 Thanksgiving meals to the homeless and less fortunate.

Introduction

Every populated area of the world relies on food from the earth to sustain its people and animals. Likewise, over time people everywhere have developed beliefs that explain why and how their crops grow or fail to grow, in turn nourishing them or letting them down. The stunning variety of crops around the world that end up on family tables are celebrated, recognized, and praised in a multitude of festivals, including the annual Thanksgiving feasts in the fall in North America and the European Midsummer celebrations on or near the longest days of the year. Some festivals are held in hopes of encouraging bountiful harvests while others celebrate a plentiful yield. Harvest festivals are often big, boisterous acknowledgments of the economic or dietary importance of certain crops to a region or group of people, such as the yam in Western Africa or sugarcane in parts of the Caribbean. Given the diversity of the world's geography and climates, during every month of the year in some part of the world, a community, village, religious group, city, or even entire country is celebrating the beginning or end of a life-giving harvest.

A family has lunch in their decorated sukkah in Zurich, Switzerland. Observant Jews live and feast in sukkahs during Sukkot, a festival honoring the harvest and the history of the early Jews.

Origins of Harvest Rites and Festivals

Since ancient people first learned that they could grow crops instead of going out to gather food, communities, towns, and entire civilizations have been able to take root. Sophisticated cultures began to develop as food drying and storage techniques allowed permanent settlements to grow into towns and cities. Over time, people also learned how to best utilize water supplies, building irrigation systems and farming techniques that worked with the land available. Soil type and quality, as well as climate, helped determine how these techniques developed and how quickly and successfully a community grew. Where there was a great lack of water, crops could not grow, and even today many of the world's arid regions remain sparsely populated. On the other hand, human ingenuity is an amazing thing, and to find proof of how advanced humans were several hundred and even 1,000 years ago, travel high up to the Inca ruins of Machu Picchu in the Andes Mountains and marvel at the ancient city surrounded by agricultural terraces watered by a system of aqueducts.

Cultivated foods and spices were eventually used as currency to trade with other communities and cultures along extensive trade routes, allowing farmers to grow even more diversified foods when traders brought back new seeds from afar. It is not an exaggeration to say that for most ancient cultures; nearly every day was devoted to working and improving the land so that its

Different Times for Harvest

Because life revolved around the growing seasons, many harvest festivals ushered in the New Year, marking the change from one harvest to the next. Others signaled the change from a time of harvest to a time when the earth is at rest. The people of the southern African country Swaziland celebrate an elaborate and lengthy harvest festival as part of their New Year, Incwala. Southern Indians celebrate their harvest festival, Pongal, in January, as do the Naga people on the border of India and Myanmar who observe Kaing Bi.

fruit, grain, and vegetable yields would sustain them through harsh winters, through droughts, through insect infestations, and through floods.

Enter the Spirits

In ancient times, people communicated with spirits and gods to satisfy urgent immediate needs, such as curing illness, avoiding danger, and securing food. Ancient civilizations often lived uncertain of what the next day or week or month might bring. Making sure to give thanks to the rain god or the spirits so that they might provide nourishment was a central part of life.

Farmers believed that spirits dwelled in crops, causing them either to thrive or die. Some cultures believed that when the fruits, grains, or vegetables were harvested, the spirits would be released to exact revenge on the farmers who had displaced them. Most early civilizations also held the belief that gods of the Sun, Moon, water, and Earth could either help humans or interfere with them and that the gods needed to be tended to constantly to make certain that the land would produce.

Ancient rituals were initiated to appease angry spirits and sometimes vengeful gods. Communities would perform rites to show the spirits that they were grateful, and they would pray to the spirits for a good agricultural season. These rites could include animal and human sacrifices, offerings of food and alcohol, and ritual dances, songs, and prayers. When ancient Egyptian farmers harvested ripe corn, they would weep and pretend to be

Shamanism in Indonesia

Still today some people believe that plants and animals have souls that can be angered. The Simatalu people on Siberut Island (located off the coast of Sumatra in Indonesia) offer chickens as sacrifice to the ancient spirits. They sing, dance, and wear colorful clothes and tattoos to make sure that the spirits that inhabit their bodies do not get bored and leave. While some of the Simatulu tribes have been Christianized, recent missionaries to the Siberut Island wear shaman beads during mass. (A shaman is a spiritual guide and healer believed to be able to divine the future.) Missionaries also attach their crosses to Siberut fetishes or objects that they believe hold spiritual power.

grief-stricken. If this was not done, the spirit they believed dwelled within the corn would supposedly become angry.

One God versus Many

Over time in many parts of the world, monotheistic religions—those that believe in one supreme god—began to replace polytheistic pagan faiths. (In this context *pagan* refers to people who do not believe in one god, but many gods who are closely connected to nature and the natural world.) Judaism, Christianity, and Islam became powerful religious systems that gradually won over pagans, either through force or gentler conversions.

Many of the old harvest rites and traditions persisted, however, and continue to be performed in some form even today. The Jewish festival Sukkot serves both to commemorate the Israelites' ancient days in the wilderness and to celebrate the ongoing harvest. In the Islamic regions of Africa, many harvest festivals are steeped in ancient spirit and ancestor worship, and dishes made from the harvest's first fruits are ritually sprinkled on the ground to please and thank the spirits. In present-day Europe, many pre-Christian autumn harvest festivals have been renamed for important saints, and European Christians and their descendants throughout the world dance with abandon around bonfires into the wee hours of the morning as their pagan ancestors did thousands of years ago.

The Purpose of Fire

Bonfires traditionally have both a festive and a practical purpose. During the Midsummer (St. John's) harvest festivals of Europe, the ashes from the all-night bonfires were regularly mixed with seed and sprinkled around the prepared fields as a form of fertilizer. In some places in Europe, such

Country Dwellers and the Roman Argot

Early peoples in Europe were collectively called "pagans," regardless of the religion they followed or the culture they were from. *Pagan* is what the Romans called them, and the Roman Catholic Church followed suit. In Latin, *paganus* means "country dweller," from the word for "country," *pagus*.

as Andorra, this rite has carried over into the present day, though it is now primarily a ceremonial blessing of the fields. Fire serves as a purification rite: burn away the old and begin anew with a fresh planting cycle.

In many cultures, flames were believed to purify by consuming or driving away evil spirits or witches. In ancient pagan Europe, fires were lit to keep away evil gods or spirits that could potentially find their way into the crops. While the belief in harmful spirits has declined, traditional bonfires continue to be held all over Europe on Midsummer night, lighting up hilltops and beaches, their flames casting flickering shadows while both young and old dance around them.

Finally, fires were also used to burn the remnants of crops after the fields were cleared, providing both an easy means of disposing of the unneeded parts and a way to celebrate the end of one cycle and the beginning of another. These traditions continue in many regions throughout the world today.

A woman prepares foods for the Yam Festival in Côte d'Ivoire. During this feast yams are celebrated as a great life-sustaining food.

Present-day Harvest Rites and Festivals with Ancient Roots

The various harvest celebrations around the world today are differentiated by the relationships that people have with the land. In Africa, harvest festivals in small villages still center on local crops that villagers rely on for survival. Many people who have moved away from their birth-villages travel back to take part in the yearly traditions and rites while relatives—often parents or grandparents—remain to farm the first fruits that are offered and eaten in these rituals. Similar practices can be found in parts of Asia, Latin America, and the Caribbean. In Cambodia, during the harvest festival Chrat Preah Nengkal, farmers offer a special meal to the cows that have plowed their fields, interpreting which foods the cows eat as a sign of how successful the harvest will be.

For most Western societies of Europe and North America, present-day harvest festivals such as Thanksgiving involve the preparing and eating of first fruits that historically grew in the regions, but most of the celebrants are no longer tied to farming, nor do they get their harvest wholly from local farms. In many parts of Europe, for the Midsummer festivals, towns and cities empty out as people travel to the countryside or the beaches. In the United States, people go en masse to supermarkets to purchase the foods necessary to make the large Thanksgiving feast, but only a small percent of the population works on farms.

Recent Harvest Festivals

Not all harvest festivals have their roots in ancient tradition. The massive sugar harvest festival Crop Over—which occurs every season when the harvesting of the sugarcane crop is over—has been celebrated in the Caribbean for only a few centuries. It began when enslaved Africans were brought over to work the cane fields. Every November 23 the people of Japan combine a traditional harvest celebration with the more modern Labor Thanksgiving Day. On this day people gather together to thank each other for their labors over the past year, as well as recognize how each person's individual labors have added to the collective wealth of the country. Most wine and beer harvest festivals celebrated near vineyards or breweries in the Americas and Europe do not have long historical traditions either. While very merry and often blessed by a local priest, these festivals—odes to the creation and consumption of regionally grown alcoholic drinks—commonly serve to attract customers to the vineyards and breweries. In South America, the introduction of wine began in the 16th century with the arrival of Spanish missionaries, and the German Oktoberfest beer bash is only two centuries old.

Beer and Sausage in Namibia

An African country might seem an unlikely place to find beer swilling and sausage making, but in Namibia it is quite common. This sparsely populated southwest African country, a former German colony, celebrates Oktoberfest along with Germany. In a country of vast deserts that is characterized by high dunes and wide open spaces, tourists and locals alike drink beer, eat sausage, and listen to German bands as if they were in Munich, Germany. To the surprise of many Anglophones, Oktoberfest is celebrated in late September.

The Yam Festival

Around 100 B.C.E. plants originally from East Asia, such as the yam, the banana, and the taro (coco yam), were introduced to Africa, although researchers are not sure how the migration took place. These plants thrived in the humid, warm rain forests of Malaysia in southeastern Asia. They did not demand tremendous labor or complex tools to cultivate, and after finding their way to Africa, they provided nutritious food for the population.

Of the many crops harvested in Africa, one of the most important is the yam. In an area known as the yam zone in Western Africa, stretching from Cameroon to Côte d'Ivoire and including Ghana and Nigeria, a full 90 percent of the world's yams are grown. This adds up to a massive 3.8 million tons of yams each year. Not only are yams important because they are exported to other countries (and so generate profits and revenue), but they are also a staple food of many African communities. For Africans, the yam has meant survival and holds an important place in the culture of numerous villages throughout the continent. In the northern region of Ghana, 75 percent of farmers cultivate yams.

The variety of yams grown in Africa is impressive. Some Africans include yams at every meal, often eating them with their hands, as has been the tradition.

Throughout the African yam zones and areas where descendants of Africans now live and grow yams, such as Haiti in the Caribbean, the yearly

Variations in Diet

Some areas of Africa were better suited than others to agricultural production. The people of the Sudan in northern Africa, for example, had numerous indigenous crops such as millet (a cereal plant), calabash (a kind of gourd), watermelon, okra, and sesame. Where there was the ability to grow foods high in nutrients and volume, populations could thrive. In other areas, for example Namibia in southern Africa, the environmental conditions did not allow for a variety of crops to grow, meaning that the development of these areas as places for people to live was much slower.

A Yam by Another Name?

In the United States, and particularly in the South, the word *yam* is often used for *sweet potato*. These two types of tubers are unrelated, though some varieties are similarly orange colored. Yams are sweeter than sweet potatoes and are native to tropical climates such as Africa and Latin America.

yam harvest begins with a celebration, a harvest festival often referred to as the New Yam Festival. It is held once a year, in August or September, just as the rainy season is ending and the yams are ripe and ready to bring in. As the villages prepare for the harvest festival activities, all old yams are eaten or thrown out to make room for the new tasty crop. Around the 10th and 11th centuries, trade brought together Muslims and traditional African communities, and for many years Muslims and African animists (tribes that believed all living things had souls and who often worshipped ancestral spirits) lived side by side in many parts of Africa.

Even when Africans converted to Islam, and later to Christianity, they found that they could believe in one god who created Heaven and Earth—a supreme deity that they understood was detached from the

Traders examine yams in a market in Bouake, Côte d'Ivoire. Nutritious and easy to grow, yams are a staple food throughout Africa.

A young boy sells yams at the side of the road in Nigeria. Yams are such an important part of people's diets that the yam harvest is an occasion for great celebrations.

day-to-day workings of a community—but still worship ancestral spirits and a multitude of gods in order to maintain harmony with the land that they needed to provide for them. To this day, while about 40 percent of the African population is Muslim (nearly all of the people in northern Africa) and about 45 percent is Christian (with larger percentages in Central and Southern Africa), most Africans also continue to worship their ancient gods and ancestors.

Communication rites continue to be carried out, especially during times of harvest. As in times past, there are traditional reasons to commune with the spirits—to make sure there will be enough food for the coming year both to sell to the larger community and for local sustenance. Harvest festivals are also a way for Africans to celebrate high yields, to relax after months of hard work in the fields, and to enjoy huge parties and food before the hard physical work must resume all over again.

(opposite page) Yams are distributed for the Yam Festival in Côte d'Ivoire.

The Moon Festival

Autumn Moon Festivals are major holidays in many Asian countries, especially China and those countries that have been heavily influenced by Chinese culture. These include Vietnam, Laos, Cambodia, Myanmar, North and South Korea, and Taiwan. While the festivals differ from country to country, and even region to region, they all take place on the day of the full Moon close to the autumn equinox (when the length of the day and the night are equal in length all over the world), which occurs at the end of September or beginning of October. Family reunions, picnics, and Moon-gazing outside in the evening with friends and relatives are a major part of the festivities. Traditionally, the Moon Festival is related to

A performing team is seen at a temple fair in Beijing, celebrating the Chinese Moon Festival.

the harvest because by this time of year the fruits, grains, and vegetables had been gathered, and there was plenty of food for everyone.

While some Asian countries today have Communist governments, such as Vietnam, North Korea, and China, that may discourage openly religious practices, many harvest traditions and festivals have persisted, and are generally not discouraged even when they involve the veneration of ancient gods. Most of the governments in the diverse countries of Asia recognize the importance of celebrating the Earth's bounty through agricultural rites associated with spirits as old as the Earth itself. In China and elsewhere, harvest festivals can serve to promote regional and national pride and to bring people together in positive nonpolitical gatherings. Also, nearly every Asian harvest festival has at its center the importance of the older generation and a family's ancestors, as children are taught about their traditions and national heritage. Respect for elders is a central element of Asian societies, and the festivals serve to support their important role in the culture.

For some East Asian countries, the autumn Moon Festivals are public holidays, meaning that businesses and schools are generally closed, and therefore families have time to get together. For others, such as China, the Moon Festival is a traditional holiday, meaning that it is widely celebrated, but business goes on as usual.

The Chinese Calendar

The Chinese calendar is lunar-based. This means that the start of the each year is determined by the cycles of the Moon. For those who follow the Chinese calendar, the beginning of the year can fall anywhere between late January and the middle of February. The calendar is also cyclical and follows a 12-year cycle. This means it repeats the same cycle every 12 years. Each year in the Chinese calendar is named for an animal, including the rooster, tiger, rabbit, or snake. The Chinese believe that people born in a particular year will possess the qualities of the animal that rules that year. For example, the year of the dog occured in 1922, 1934, 1946, 1958, 1970, 1982, 1994, and 2006. Those born during these years are believed to be loyal and honest, but they can also be selfish and odd.

Respecting Elders in the East

Much of East Asian culture's focus on respect for elders and authority can be traced back to Confucius (known as Master Kong among East Asians), who lived from 551 to 479 B.C.E. Famous for his ideas about education, philosophy, and politics, Confucius believed in showing restraint when speaking, refraining from criticizing one's government, showing the utmost admiration for family elders, and respecting customs and good manners. Today throughout the world, his pithy sayings are well known and often recited. Among them are:

- "I hear and I forget. I see and I remember. I do and I understand."
- "Our greatest glory is not in never falling, but in getting up every time we do."
- "He who speaks without modesty will find it difficult to make his words good."
- "Ignorance is the night of the mind, but a night without Moon and star."
- "Ignorance is the night of the mind, but a night without Moon and star."

China's Early Interest in the Moon

Evidence suggests that ancient China showed intense and early interest in the Moon, carefully recording its motion. These recordings became part of astrological thought. Ancient Chinese observations were so precise that they could predict when eclipses would occur. Eclipses occur when a planet or other astronomical body such as the Sun is blocked from view because a different object (such as the Moon) comes between the observer and the body. Not surprisingly, the Moon is a prominent figure in the oral traditions of the Chinese, as well as those of surrounding cultures that have historically been under the influence or direct control of China.

Worshipping the Harvest Moon

For thousands of years, stories have been passed down about the Moon goddess, Chango-Er, and how she came to live in the Moon. The most

In Seoul, South Korea, children in traditional Korean holiday dress jump rope, which is a traditional game played during the Chusok Full Moon Harvest Festival.

popular story is that the famous archer Hou Yi was asked by the emperor of China to shoot down nine of the 10 suns that were burning the Earth and threatening to extinguish all of humanity. Yi shot down the nine suns and was rewarded with a pill that would grant him eternal life. His wife, Chango-Er, found the pill and swallowed it first. When Yi found out, he went to reprimand her. However, filled with double the prescribed dosage of immortality, she floated up from the Earth all the way to the surface of the Moon where she still lives today. Once a year, on the 15th day of the full Moon, Yi visits his wife. That is why the Moon is full and beautiful on that night.

Chinese autumn Moon worship is thought to have begun around 1,000 B.C.E. and gained popularity around 500 C.E. The round full Moon is a symbol of coming together for the Chinese, and on this day every month families all over East Asia will reunite if they have been apart, or spend time thinking of one another if they are unable to be together. They burn incense as an offering to Chango-Er, hoping that she will protect them in their coming harvest.

The Midsummer's Day/St. John's Day Festival

The Summer Solstice Brings Light and Laughter

In the part of the world known today as Europe, summer harvest festivals were originally fertility rituals, performed to make certain that the first fruits of the farmers' labors would be plentiful and sustain them through the coming winter. This would be no small achievement because Europeans, especially in the North, had to endure a hard and dark winter. The ancient tribes of Northern Europe were probably scared when the

People dance around a bonfire during the ancient night-long celebration marking the summer solstice, the shortest night of the year, in Belarus. St. John's Day or Midsummer's Day celebrations center around bonfires with plenty of food and dancing.

Sunlight and the Axis

In the regions located north of the Arctic Circle and south of the Antarctic Circle, the Sun shines continuously longer than anywhere else on Earth. This day, called a polar day, can last for six months at the North Pole. This phenomenon occurs because the Earth is tilted on its axis, and at these extreme latitudes, the Sun remains above the horizon even after setting. The opposite phenomenon, known as polar night, occurs in these regions when the Sun remains below the horizon, even after rising. The farther the observer moves away from the poles, the shorter the duration of these phenomena.

Sun would go down for such long periods of time, worrying that it would never return again. However, when the Sun shone later into the evening during the short summer, these early farmers wanted to do everything to show the powerful force of nature that they were grateful for the Sun's presence. They needed its light to help them provide food for their families to survive the long dark months to come. Like African animists, the ancient Europeans also believed that spirits lived in the crops, and that the spirits would need to be thanked and placated if they as a people were to survive. In these ancient times, when day-to-day survival was often a struggle, the joyous Midsummer's Day traditions were born.

Northern Europe, especially close to the Arctic Circle, can be an icy place marked by long dark nights and short frigid days. In the northern-most parts of Finland, Sweden, and Norway, the Sun does not rise for more than 50 days during the dead of winter, and darkness is cast over the sparsely inhabited lands. During the short summer, when the Sun does not go far below the horizon, however, these Scandinavian countries experience the opposite occurrence, and it will often still be sunny at 11:00 at night. These long days last for more than two months of the summer and are a welcome change from the cold and long winter.

Magical Midsummer's Eve

On or near the eve of the summer solstice, great gatherings would take place to celebrate the summer, to perform ceremonial dances and chants in an attempt to ensure good coming harvests, and to try to influence the future with magic elixirs and herbs. (The summer solstice is the longest day of the year, when the Sun is farthest from the equator.) Pre-Christian Europeans believed that the eve of the summer solstice was a night of magic when herbs were at their most powerful and should be picked for their healing powers. The summer solstice occurs in the middle of the welcome summer (which is how the Midsummer festival got its name).

As in many other early societies, medieval Europeans believed that spirits dwelled within the crops and caused these crops to live or die. Rites were performed to help get rid of the spirits or to keep them away, so that the fall harvest would sustain the people. On the eve of the summer solstice, pagans would build a huge bonfire to keep the spirits away and out of the crops. Bonfires had multiple meanings during Midsummer festivals, and one tradition that continues today is jumping over smaller bonfires on this night for good luck. As in other cultures, the bonfires also drew, and still draw, people together, who dance and sing around the flames from Midsummer's eve to the next morning.

Midsummer's Day Gets a Second Name

These magical harvest festivals were looked down on by medieval Christians passionate in their desire to convert the pagans to Christianity. Ultimately, the fervent early Christians were successful in converting pagans to one Christian God, but the process was a slow one. To take control of animist practices, they renamed the harvest festivals for the early Christian martyr St. John, who was an apostle. (A martyr is someone who dies for the for the cause of his or her faith or belief.) His birthday was celebrated on June 24, a day that fell on or close to the summer solstice. This day was designated as St. John's Day, a feast day for the saint. (A feast day is a day when saints or important Catholics are remembered in special ways and thanked for their contributions.) Sometimes St. John's Day might include a communal meal. By renaming, instead of forbidding, the harvest practices, the Catholics ensured that these agricultural festivals and some of their accompanying traditions would continue. Today, whether it is known as Midsummer's Day or St. John's Day, this harvest festival is one of the most important holidays in northern Europe, second only to Christmas.

A Bavarian waitress carries beer at Oktoberfest, the world's biggest beer festival, in Munich, Germany.

The Fall Harvest Festivals of Europe

In some countries harvest festivals are celebrated in the fall, rather than in midsummer. These festivals often reveal roots both pagan and Christian. Some began during the early Christian era when Roman Catholic priests and their saints held religious sway over the majority of Europeans. In Europe, some fall harvest festivals are also saints' days with elaborate feasts and stories surrounding the saints, such as St. Leopold's Day in Austria and St. Martin's Day in Denmark. Austria's St. Leopold's Day and the wildly popular German Oktoberfest are harvest festivals that revel in the role that wine and beer play in the culture and economy. However, the ancient pagan rites that took place during the fall to mark the change of seasons have also found a place in these festivities, such as the lighting of fires and lanterns during St. Martin's Day in numerous countries throughout Europe.

Sukkot

A Harvest Festival with Roots in Early Judaism

The festival of Sukkot (also called the Feast of Tabernacles or Feast of Booths) honors the harvest and the history of the early Jews during the 40 years after they left Egypt and wandered in the wilderness before they found their way to their promised land. It is a joyous festival that comes after the very solemn series of observances in the fall, a time when Jews observe the New Year of Rosh Hashanah and repent and make amends for their past sins during Yom Kippur. After these deeply reflective and often solemn High Holy Days, Sukkot allows families to rejoice and thank god for their many blessings.

Sukkot is both a harvest and a historical festival that falls between the end of September and the middle of October every year. It takes place on the 15th through the 21st of Tishri, the seventh month of the Jewish calendar. Like many festivals celebrated by Jews, there is a connection to the early Hebrews; both their role in creating Judaism and sustaining the Jewish faith through very difficult times. The Hebrew Bible (which also forms the longest part of the Christion Bible, The Old Testament) mentions Sukkot as one of three pilgrimage harvest festivals and commands that Jews celebrate for seven days by building sukkots, or temporary huts (also known as tabernacles or booths), and living and feasting in them to better

A Jewish worshipper holds the four species of plants that are used in rituals during the Jewish holiday of Sukkot during a special blessing at the Western Wall, Judaism's holiest prayer site, in Jerusalem.

understand their ancestors' time of wandering, following their exodus from Egypt. The connection to the harvest is shown by decorating the sukkah with anything that grows in the ground. It also reminds Jews of the early farming tradition of taking the first fruits of the fall crops to the Jewish Temple, where they were given as offerings to god.

Preparing for the Harvest Feast

Before the first eve of Sukkot, wherever Jews live, families put together their three-sided huts, using branches for temporary roofs. Observant Jews (those who regularly take part in religious rituals and obey their faith's religious commandments) in Israel, the United States, Canada, Mexico, and Europe, among other countries, put up their sukkah on back porches, on balconies, and in yards. The building of sukkah for the holiday also recalls the practice of ancient farmers constructing temporary huts near their fields in which to sleep during the harvest of grapes,

A Jewish family relaxes in their decorated sukkah in Zurich, Switzerland. The sukkah is made of natural materials and is built in the garden, in the courtyard, or on the balcony. Observant Jews are supposed to make an effort to live in the hut during the seven- to eight-day Sukkot festival in autumn, including eating, praying, celebrating, and sleeping there.

olives, grain, and other crops. Afterward, to show their gratitude for having enough to sustain themselves through the coming winter, ancient Jews would travel to the Temple in Jerusalem to thank god for their blessings. (Jerusalem is one of the most ancient cities in the world and is holy to Christians, Jews, and Muslims.) Because of this historical harvest offering, Jews today bring palm fronds, myrtle boughs, citron, and willow branches to be blessed after Sukkot. These ceremonial objects have come to be known as the four species.

A sukkah must have three walls and be strong enough to stay up even in strong winds. The roof, put on last, must not be tied down and must be made with material grown in the ground—reeds, branches from trees, willows, or cornstalks are often used. Before meals in the Sukkot, Jews recite the following prayer

Blessed are You,
Our God, Creator of time and space,
who enriches our lives with holiness,
commanding us to dwell in the sukkah.

As for the Sukkot meal itself, there are no strict rules for what Jews should eat during this celebration. However, foods that are stuffed, such as peppers and eggplants, are common. Often they are stuffed with other vegetables, a representation of the first fruits that historically were part of this harvest tradition. For certain, on most plates during Sukkot, a participant will find a lot of fresh fruits and vegetables.

Americans are often surprised by how similar the holiday of Sukkot is to Thanksgiving. It is believed today that the deeply Christian American Pilgrims, from whom Americans get their historical harvest festival, looked to the Bible and based Thanksgiving at least in part on descriptions of Sukkot found in the Hebrew Bible.

Latin American Harvest Festivals

European Encounters with a New People, New Cultures, and Tasty Fare

Latin Americans have been giving thanks for abundant harvests for thousands of years, well before the arrival of Italian explorer Christopher Columbus (or Cristóbal Colón, as he is known in Latin America). More than 500 years ago, when Columbus and other early colonizers first stepped onto the shores of the area that comprises Central and South America and the Caribbean, there were already sophisticated farming systems in place. Though foreign and exotic to the eyes of the explorers, a large number of crops such as beans, cacao, squash, corn, peanuts, gourds, and peppers were already staples throughout parts of Latin America.

While the early Spanish explorers arrived already hungry for the precious gold and silver that adorned the royalty of the Aztec and Inca civilizations, they also found some mouth-watering new foods that proved irresistible. Chocolate, used to make a spicy, sugarless drink by the Maya and the Aztec who lived in what is today Mexico and Guatemala, was soon to find its way onto the plates and into the cups of the upper ranks of Spanish and European society. The Spanish explorers were surely impressed by the crops that the "New World" had to offer, just as they must have been astonished to discover the elaborate food storage facilities of the Aztec, or the terrace farming techniques of the Inca and other South American civilizations.

For Sweets, Try Adding Sugar

The word *chocolate* comes from the Nahuatl word *xocoatl*, which means "bitter water." Initially the cocoa bean was too bitter for Spanish tastes, but when the Spaniards experimented with the bean by adding cane sugar, a new delicacy was born. This new sweetened chocolate was loved by the Spanish aristocracy, and eventually consumed all over Europe, including at the royal courts of France.

The indigenous tribes of what is now Peru had discovered how to take land that was seemingly impossible to cultivate and, with remarkable engineering skills, create irrigation systems that carried water to the heights of mountains and through sophisticated cities, such as the remarkable Machu Picchu (where the royal estate of the Sapa Inca, the Inca ruler, was located). By the time the Spanish conquistadores arrived, the Aztecs had already converted the swampland located where Mexico City stands today into remarkable floating gardens called *chinampas*. Their techniques continue to be studied and imitated to this day.

New Christian Names for Ancient Harvest Festivals

Similar to the Spaniards' own Catholic society, the Aztec and Inca had highly organized religious communities with priests and places of worship. They had developed stratified social systems with royalty on the top

Aztec dancers perform ancient harvest rites in Mexico. The Aztec civilization dominated modern-day Mexico and when it was conquered by the Spaniards, many of its festivals, including those connected to the harvest, were renamed by the Catholic Spanish.

Aztecs' Special Regard for the Different

Aztec children of the noble class attended religious schools called *calmecacs*. These schools for boys were physically and mentally challenging, as they were the training grounds for future priests and office holders. Some of the rigors included bloodletting, fasts, and learning to care for the temple lands. The boys also were schooled in dream interpretation, astrology, and understanding the calendar. Girls attended separate *calmecacs* and learned to be skilled weavers and embroiderers. They were cared for inside the temple school by priestesses, and some who did not marry stayed inside the walls and became priestesses themselves.

and in which the commoners did the menial tasks of the community. However, a major difference between the Europeans of 500 years ago and the indigenous civilizations they encountered was the way that they prayed and gave thanks to their gods. As with the ancient Romans, many of the Latin American indigenous religious rites were essentially harvest rituals enacted to keep their often perilous physical world in harmony.

Some indigenous groups of Latin America made ritualistic animal and human sacrifices to their gods, believing that they would then be granted plentiful crops for the coming season. The people of ancient Latin America revered their gods, but like the early Europeans, they also feared them. They felt that their gods needed to be fed regularly in order to be kept satisfied. In what is present-day Mexico, the Aztec made seasonal human and animal sacrifices to many gods, among them Tlaloc, the god of rain, fertility, and water. Since Aztecs believed Tlaloc was responsible for floods and drought, many sacrificial ceremonies were required to keep him happy.

By the 16th century in most of Europe, harvest festival sacrifices no longer required the actual spilling of blood. For Christians, the sacrifice was symbolic, as was shown in church communion rites. Communion in the Catholic and Protestant Churches was, and is, a rite where the priest or church authority asks the congregants to focus on their prophet Jesus' sacrifice on the cross by feeding them bits of crackers, or bread, and wine, or juice, to symbolize the body and blood of Jesus.

While the early conquistadores were fairly successful in eliminating human sacrifice in harvest festivals in the Americas (though they often employed violent measures themselves, such as requiring the conquered to convert or be killed), their attempts to wipe out the festivals themselves were unsuccessful. When it was clear that they could not eradicate the festivals, early Christians worked to transfer the focus of the harvest celebrations from many gods to one Christian God. One way they did this was by renaming festivals using names that honored Catholic saints, such as St. John the Baptist, especially if the ceremonies occurred around the same time of year.

Indigenous Pride Grows in Latin America

During the middle and late 20th century, after many years of Spanish dominance, a new pride began to grow throughout the indigenous community, especially in countries such as Peru and Guatemala that still have large indigenous populations. The Incas initially regarded themselves highly, as they considered themselves to be children of the Sun. However, once separated from social and political power, their empire fell apart. In the 20th century, along with their newly restored pride came the understanding of rich pre-Columbian traditions. While a huge majority of Latin Americans are deeply Catholic, the ancient gods and rituals continue to find their place in present-day harvest festivals, not always in spite of the Catholic saints, but sometimes alongside them.

Thanksgiving

Harvest Celebrations in a Not-So-New Land

When Europeans first arrived in what is today North America, they brought with them their own harvest festival traditions from their old countries. In England, Spain, and all over Europe harvest festivals with roots in ancient pagan traditions were held before and after harvest cycles to give thanks to God for a good produce, to rejoice together after much hard work, and to cook and eat special harvest foods with family and friends. To feel at home in a strange new land meant that early settlers in today's Canada and the United States would often re-create these traditions, over time changing them as they learned about their new land and what would grow there. From the beginning, their understanding was improved by their early interactions with indigenous tribes who intimately knew the land.

At the same time, Native American tribes who had been on the continent for more than 12,000 years and numbered in the millions also celebrated the beginning and ending of harvest seasons through numerous rites, customs, and traditions. Among them were the Anasazi, the Inuit the Mound Builders, the Sioux Nations (Lakota, Dakota, and Nakota), and the Six Nations, or Iroquois Confederacy. Native rites and dances were performed to please spirits that dwelled in the corn, pumpkin, and beans, just to name a few. Many tribes believed that most animal-related illnesses could be cured with plant-based remedies.

Plants were revered among tribes, who knew that their survival was intimately tied to the health of the land. Perhaps the most important of these crops was corn, as it was highly nutritious and did not require huge amounts of hard labor to grow. Corn, beans, and squash could also be dried and stored for long periods of time, which allowed the American Indians to go on long hunting and war expeditions, as well as providing them with time to trade with other tribes.

When Native Americans and European settlers met one another during the 16th and 17th centuries, the meetings were often marked by suspicion on both sides. For good reason indigenous tribes often distrusted the intentions of the British colonists and other early settlers. Colonists believed this new world to be theirs for the taking, using their religion to justify removing lands from tribes up and down the eastern coasts of

Regrouping for Strength

As the numbers of American Indian tribes in the United States dwindled, many joined together and formed new federations, which allowed for some bargaining power after European descendants took control of the land and formed new governments. It also brought together groups that celebrated similar harvest festivals. Many of these festivals continue to be celebrated today.

North America. Through force and treaty, early Europeans, with their backing from England and France, took lands and livelihood from the tribes. In addition to the forcible removal of land, indigenous people also became sickened by diseases such as smallpox brought over by the colonists. Millions died in the first decades of contact between Europeans and the tribes of the Americas. Today there are still small communities with ancient roots in North America that live both within and outside of Indian reservations throughout the United States and Indian reserves throughout Canada, but in numbers nowhere near the millions that populated the continent for thousands of years.

In recent years, Canada has worked to make amends to the Native American groups who lost their land and independence as French and British settlers took over their territory. In 1998, the government apologized to the groups for 150 years of abuse and in 1999 the vast territory of Nunavut (which means "Our Land") was carved out of Canada's Northwest Territories province as a homeland for the Inuit nation.

Some early meetings in North America are memorable not for conflict but for harmony. The United States and Canadian Thanksgiving celebrations today are a result of positive early interactions between Native Americans and early settlers, even if many North American chroniclers have romanticized these early meetings to elevate the people who came to be known as Pilgrims. These early communal gatherings give present-day descendants of the early settlers to Canada and the United States their most widely celebrated Thanksgiving harvest festivals, known in both countries as Thanksgiving. Though the majority of Canadians and Americans celebrate the holiday, the Canadians do not

A Native American woman turns ducks on a spit during a recreation of the harvest feast at Plymouth, Massachusetts, which eventually became Thanksgiving.

specifically recognize the contributions of the English colonists who landed at Plymouth, Massachusetts.

Origins of North American Thanksgiving

Canada and the United States celebrate the holiday of Thanksgiving in the fall. In both countries, days of thanksgiving were first celebrated in the colonial period, and came from the same European traditions. These thanksgiving traditions originated in European countries to show appreciation for successful voyages, peace, and, of course, abundant harvests. In Canada, Thanksgiving falls on the second Monday in October and, in the United States, on the fourth Thursday in November.

Tree Sap and a National Symbol

Long before Europeans entered Canada, First Nations peoples discovered the food properties of maple sap, which they gathered every spring. As early as 1700, the maple leaf was serving as Canada's national symbol. In 1965, it was incorporated into Canada's flag. Today all over Canada in the early Spring are maple festivals complete with maple syrup demonstrations, snowshoe races, craft shows, and dancing and singing, just to name a few. Because it is sure to be chilly, the best part might be the pancake breakfasts with fresh sausage and pancakes smothered with fresh and local maple syrup.

Martin Frobisher Arrives in 1578

In 1578, Canada celebrated its first Thanksgiving, initiated by the English navigator and explorer Martin Frobisher. Frobisher had made several attempts to find a northern route to Asia but never succeeded. His third attempt was cut short by storms and icy water. After being driven to the shores of the modern-day province of Newfoundland, Canada, he held a ceremony to give thanks for surviving the long journey across the Atlantic Ocean. Years later, this tradition was continued by settlers in that region. Thanksgiving in the United States, commemorating the Massachusetts Bay Colony's first harvest in 1621, also influenced Canada's holiday, as colonists loyal to Britain brought the tradition to Canada when they left the American colonies in advance of the American Revolution (1775–1783).

Plymouth Colony, 1621

It had been a truly difficult year for the first Pilgrims after making it across the Atlantic in the cold December of 1620. They had not enough to eat or drink, and nearly half of the 102 new immigrants would die the first winter. These men and women were both deeply pious and terrified people who anticipated that danger awaited them in the form of indigenous

From "First Comer" to "Pilgrim"

The Plymouth colonists were not generally called Pilgrims until 1863. Though they considered themselves pilgrims toward heavenly bliss, for their outward name, they were called Separatists—pious Christians who fled an oppressive environment in England and found English investors to help them set up a colony in the "New World." They sometimes called themselves *pilgrims* as a way of connecting their colonizing experience with that of the Hebrews in order to identify themselves as God's chosen people. Until the late 18th century they were called either Old Comers or First Comers. By the time President Abraham Lincoln named Thanksgiving as a national holiday in 1863, their success and founding status made the term *Pilgrim* better suited than the older names.

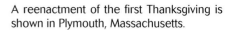
A reenactment of the first Thanksgiving is shown in Plymouth, Massachusetts.

people, as well as starvation. Yet, they had made it to a new land, where they hoped to find the freedom to worship their god the way they could not in Europe.

On March 16, 1621, a Native American boy approached the Pilgrims' settlement, at first frightening them, until he greeted them by saying, "welcome" in English. His name was Samoset, and he had learned English from captains of fishing boats that used to sail off the coast. Samoset later introduced the Pilgrims to Squanto, who was even more fluent in English (he had spent considerable time in Spain and England). Squanto's value to the Pilgrims was immense, and the Pilgrims probably would not have survived without his knowledge and help. He taught them to tap maple trees for sap, as well as how to hunt and the best places to fish. He taught them about specific local plants' medicinal qualities and about those that were poisonous. He showed them how to plant Indian corn by

A Sad Anniversary

Since 1970, Native Americans and supporters have held a National Day of Mourning at Plymouth Rock in Plymouth, Massachusetts, to protest the U.S. government's history of overlooking the rights and dignity of Native American tribes.

piling the earth into several low mounds with fish and seeds in each one so that the decaying fish would fertilize the corn. Squanto also taught them to plant a variety of crops with the corn, resulting in an abundant harvest in the fall for the Pilgrims. In gratitude, the Pilgrims held a harvest feast, lasting three days, and invited the neighboring Native Americans to share the celebration with them. These early settlers, having come from England where they were accustomed to celebrating the harvest with feasts of thanksgiving, probably wanted to continue the tradition in this new land.

Attending this first feast was not only Squanto but also chief Massasoit, leader of the Wampanoag and the person who would soon establish a 50-year-long peace treaty with the colonists. Historic evidence today suggests that the Pilgrims' invitation, while genuine, was also intended to be a show of force, so that their new neighbors might fear and respect them. During the three-day harvest feast, while thanking the Lord for his goodness, the colonists also spent a good deal of time shooting off English muskets. This may not have been the first Thanksgiving in the country—thanksgiving services were routine in what was to become the state of Virginia as early as 1607—but it was nonetheless an impressive one.

Thanksgiving Becomes Official

The historic day in 1621 at Plymouth Colony in New England that Americans associate with Thanksgiving was never intended to be a permanent harvest celebration. In fact, historic records show that by 1621 up north in Canada and as far south as Florida, where the Spanish colonists lived, there had already been several harvest celebrations of thanksgiving. However, it is this one particular feast that schoolchildren all over the United States have been taught to associate with the Thanksgiving dinners indulged in today by nearly all people from the United States (and wherever Americans have permanently settled in large numbers). It is a good story, so it is not surprising that Americans hang on to this one harvest celebration to explain their modern holiday. After being celebrated regionally off and on for a couple of centuries, Thanksgiving was declared a national U.S. holiday by President Abraham Lincoln in 1863 during the Civil War in an attempt to foster unity between the North and South, and set on the final Thursday of November. The date for this Thanksgiving was formally set on the next to last Thursday by President Roosevelt in 1939. Because the 1930s was a time of what is now known as the Great

Thanksgiving Far and Wide

Since 1870, Liberia, a Western African country, has celebrated the first Thursday in November as Thanksgiving Day. It is an important holiday for Liberians, and all public and private institutions are closed on this day. Liberia's Thanksgiving celebrates when it became an independent nation. Additionally, many Liberians emigrated from the United States, where Thanksgiving is an important holiday.

Thanksgiving is also celebrated in parts of Oceania in the Pacific Ocean, in the countries of Palau and the Marshall Islands (which were under U.S. administration for a very long time) and in Samoa (part of which is still under United States control).

Depression (a time of great economic hardship for most of the population of the United States), Roosevelt wanted to give merchants a little longer to sell their products before Christmas. In 1941 congress formally set the federal Thanksgiving holiday to occur on the fourth Thursday in November annually.

Canada's first official Thanksgiving holiday was celebrated on April 5, 1872, because the Prince of Wales had recovered from a serious illness. In 1879 Parliament declared Thanksgiving a national holiday. The date has changed over the years, until it took its current place on the calendar as the second Monday of October in 1957. Canadian Thanksgiving takes place in October, presumably because it is colder earlier there, and the crops have annually been harvested by October.

(*opposite page*) *Collier's* a weekly magazine founded in 1888 by bookseller Peter F. Collier, began as an illustrated journal with a liberal editorial policy. By the 20th century *Collier's* gained a wider audience when it began publishing sports and celebrity news along with literary fiction. This issue, published in 1901, commemorates Thanksgiving before it fell on a fixed date.

Dancers wear elaborate costumes during a festival in a small Andean village in Ecuador. The masks, which can weigh up to 20 pounds, are worn by male dancers as part of festivities that combine the Roman Catholic feast of Corpus Christi with traditional Indian harvest celebrations.

Regional Traditions and Customs

◎ ◎ ◎

Africa

Culture, Land, and Climate on a Vast Continent

Africa is a colossal continent. It holds 22 percent of the Earth's land surfaces, and the United States would easily fit inside its Sahara desert. Within Africa are the far-reaching Congo and Niger rivers, as well as the world's longest river, the Nile. The continent extends on both sides of the equator with deserts making up 40 percent of the continent. Only 8 percent of the land is covered in rain forest. The savannas, which are open plains and grasslands, extend between these deserts and forests, and in good times (when there is enough rain) plant life flourishes there.

However, harmful bacteria and disease-carrying insects also thrive on the continent, since the climate is generally warm and without seasonal differences. There are no winter frosts to remove the potential dangers provided by insects and bacteria. Life in many parts of Africa has always been precarious for animals and humans alike. It is within these conditions that African community life developed, and religions evolved. Basic survival required keeping the natural world in harmony.

Elders, Ancestral Spirits, Drums, and Yams

The New Yam Festivals, Homowo and Incwala, are colorful and joyous harvest festivals with a multitude of rites, traditions, and foods. While customs are not identical from city to town to small village, they all celebrate the harvest of

A woman prepares food for the annual Yam Festival in Côte d'Ivoire.

the all-important yam. Most villages forbid anyone to eat the newly harvested yams until the village elder or king has been given a specially prepared yam to taste. This individual is believed to be the go-between for the community and the gods; because of his importance for the tribe or community and the respect he commands, he is the most suitable member to communicate the tribe's appreciation to the gods for making the yam. Other common traditions during yam harvest festivals include providing yam offerings to a deceased family member or to tribal ancestors. Ancestor worship is common in Africa, and most tribes believe that relatives who have died serve as superior messengers to the spirits. Drumming, dancing, wearing colorful and specially chosen clothing, and athletic events are also part of most yam harvest festivals. Most importantly, African harvest festivals embrace feasting on the first fruits that allow a community to continue to exist in a sometimes dangerous, hungry and uncertain world.

Unique Customs and Traditions

Yams and Homecomings in Ghana

In Ghana, a West African country between Côte d'Ivoire and Togo, yams are a way of life. Most farmers plant at least five different kinds of yams, and many have specific cultural purposes. The Chenchito yam is consumed during funerals and festivals, for instance, while the smaller Kpuringa

A warrior of the Ga tribe celebrates the annual Homowo (hooting at hunger) festival in Accra, Ghana.

yams are usually eaten by children. The yam called Baayeri is held to be the leader of all yam types. Farmers believe that if they do not have some Baayeri yams in their fields, the other yam types will leave the farm, never to return.

The Dagomba tribes, most of whom live in northern Ghana, celebrate the New Yam harvest feasts by serving yams with fish, chicken, or lamb, as well as with pumpkin, corn, and African greens. At the start of the festival, women dig up yams from the fields and carry them home in baskets on their heads. Every yam farming family wants to be the one with the largest crop. The village comes together as the women and girls of the community prepare the feast. Often a young boy of the village is chosen to carry the best yams to the dinner, followed by others who beat drums and march to the festivities. The village chiefs also follow the yams, wearing dramatic Ghanaian kente cloth and everyone sings. Some villagers might also wear masks that represent the harvest gods while dancing to the diverse drums made from calabash (a kind of gourd) or clay pots and other materials. The villagers believe that through the masqueraders they can communicate directly with the different harvest gods.

Another Ghanaian festival that includes the valued yam as well as celebrates all local crops is called Homowo. This word means to "hoot at hunger," or to make fun of it. The oral history of this tribe of the southern Accra Plains describes a deadly famine that befell the Ga people long ago. (Today the Ga people make up about 8 percent of Ghana's population.) When it was over, the Ga people were so incredibly relieved and joyful that they began cultivating their land in earnest, which soon led to huge harvests. Over time, relief and exuberance at having enough to eat became formalized in a festival that would mock hunger. While the ceremonial customs and rites are not exactly the same for every village or tribe, the festival generally starts in May when there are light rains and local priests plant grain crops such as millet and corn. The festival culminates in August (the exact date depends on the Ga priests who must turn for counsel to oracles, visions, and prophecies).

Between May and August, many diverse traditions take place that vary from village to village. In most places, a ban on noise is established, especially drumming and sing-ing. Also, other activities such as fishing are limited. In some communities, the clubs and dance halls are closed. The bans enable the gods to focus on ensuring an abundant harvest in peace and quiet. In early August, the Ga people celebrate a yam festival in honor of the Ga spirits that protect them. All Ga people must return to their fathers' homes during the appointed time in August. Thousands of people travel hundreds of miles to their Ga villages and cities to take part in Homowo rites and festivities. Those who come from nearby villages often bring their newly harvested crops with them, including pepper, onions, corn, and okra. These nearby villages, now with locals and relatives from far away, are the sites of parades and musical fes-tivities. Also during Homowo, relatives who have died over the past year are given a memorial service, and loud wailing echoes through the streets and homes. There is also a birthday celebration for all of the twins and multiple births during the past year, since twins are venerated by the Ga people and considered exceptional blessings.

Homowo day itself, which changes date from year to year as it is based on the Ga priests' oracles, is a day of food, especially a fermented corn meal dish known as *kpekpele* (also called *kpokpoi*), a kind of a fish stew that is made with palm oil, corn dough, and okra. The *kpekpele* is sprinkled by each city's chief at sacred places in order to please the gods and ancestors. The head of every household will also sprinkle *kpekpele* in places special to the individual families or to the tribes, such as in front of their homes or the homes of the village priests. After the rituals are performed, the joy-ous dancing and drumming begins in the streets and during this celebra-tion everyone is equal in social standing. During Homowo, the Ga people often welcome visitors and even strangers into their homes to share a traditional meal. Right after Homowo, which can last a few days or more

Spirited Harvest Recipes

The Dagomba people of Ghana believe that gods dwell in the stones and trees, and if boiled yams with herbs are rubbed on the stones, they will ensure the goodwill of the deities.

Twins and Yams!

West Africa has a remarkable number of twins born annually compared to the rest of the world. This is especially true for Nigeria's Yoruba tribe. A full 5 percent of all births produce twins (compared to half of 1 percent for the rest of the world). Since twins are considered a blessing and an omen of good luck, the Yoruba take much pride in their twins. In a small farming community called Igbo-Ora in southwest Nigeria, a sign proclaiming it as The Land of Twins welcomes visitors. Some experts believe that regular yam consumption is one reason for the high rate of twin births. (Yams contain a hormone that can cause the ovaries to produce an egg from each side.)

than a week in different regions, the Ga celebrate a day of remembrance to honor loved ones who have died during the past year. This is also the day when the Ga resolve disputes, if they are feuding with others, and arrange marriages.

Incwala (Festival of First Fruits) in Swaziland

In the tiny country between South Africa and Mozambique a gigantic six-day celebration is held that is a harvest festival, an annual ceremony that renews the strength of the Swazi king, and that also serves as a New Year celebration. It is the most sacred ceremony for the Swazi and is usually performed in December or January (astrologers decide the exact date after a thorough study of planetary movements). Before the celebration, the king isolates himself from the rest of the tribe while a chosen group of learned men known as Bemanti (Swazi water officials) travel to the Indian Ocean off Mozambique to collect the foam of the ocean waves. This foam is believed to have medicinal and mystical powers. Their return to Swaziland marks the beginning of the main celebration, called Incwala or Festival of First Fruits.

Adolescents from all over the country gather at the royal kraal (kraals are huts in which indigenous South Africans live), where the king orders them to collect branches of a shrub called *lusekwane*; the elders then use the branches to build a sacred hut for the king. Swazi warriors, wearing ox hides and leopard skins, dance throughout the ceremony and request the king to join in their celebrations.

On the fourth day of the ceremony, the king ends his seclusion. His body is covered with bright green grass, his face is blackened, and he wears a silver-colored monkey-skin belt around his waist. His headdress is made up of large black plumes and feathers from the sakabula bird (a long-tailed widowbird; *sakabula* is a Swazi word that means "show-off" or "flirt"). The king dances with the warriors while the queen mother looks after the guests. The king eats a portion of a pumpkin—*luselwa* in Swazi—specially kept aside for this ceremony. The remaining *luselwa* is then tossed toward the warriors, symbolizing that the king has now had the first fruit and the locals can now consume their new crops.

On the fifth day of the festival, a day of rest, no activity takes place. For the sixth and final day of Incwala, the Swazi light a grand bonfire and burn articles that represent the past year. The king and his people pray to the ancestral spirits to smother the fire by sending down rains. If the rains come, the Swazi believe the New Year will be a good one. On the last day, everyone dances and eats. The ceremony ends after the successful weeding of the king's fields by the Swazi youth.

Asia

Rural Asia, Monsoons, and Crops

When Asia is in the news, it is often for its immense urban areas of India and China, Japan and Korea, and for such cities as Beijing, Tokyo, Seoul, and New Delhi. In fact, six out of 10 of the world's most populous countries are in Asia (China, India, Indonesia, Pakistan, Bangladesh and Japan).

However, even today more than half of Asia's population still lives in rural areas. While this is expected to change throughout this century, in China, Korea, India, Japan, and other Asian countries, a large percentage of people continue to live in small villages and work on farms, as they have for centuries, feeding their families and trying to survive through the good and bad harvests.

Rowing enthusiasts participate in a dragon boat race as part of celebrations marking the Moon Festival in Hong Kong.

A performer jumps through a ring of fire during a fair to celebrate the Moon Festival in Singapore. The festival began as a Harvest Moon celebration in ancient China.

Since Asia has a remarkable variety in climate and geography, many kinds of crops are grown. For example, in South Asia, monsoons bring cold dry air in the winter and warm moist air in the summer, releasing rains. In the wettest areas, rice is grown, and wheat and other grains are the major crops in the drier areas. Asia supplies the world with 90 percent of its rice, and this important crop occupies more land than any other grown in Asia. Other important crops include wheat, soybeans, barley, and corn, as well as cotton and tea (usually grown as cash crops on large plantations).

The Role of Fire

As in Africa, in Asia ancient traditions play a central role in the many diverse harvest festivals that stretch from August to January throughout this vast continent. In some of the festivals such as Pongal in India, the Moon Festivals in Vietnam and in Macau and Hong Kong in China, and the Naga New Year festival in Myanmar, fire is seen as an illuminating and purifying force and plays an important part in the celebrations. Bonfires are common during these thanksgiving festivals, as are the making and displaying of lanterns. In Macau, lanterns are placed in bodies of water during the full Moon, creating beautiful shimmering reflections as hundreds of them float away together. In ancient times, these intricate lanterns were a way to commune with the water gods. Today, people in Macau might write their wishes on the small and lovely lanterns before setting them free. In Vietnam, families make the lanterns together and participate in lantern contests and parades.

Water and Water Gods

The theme of water comes up again and again during many Asian harvest festivals, especially during the Onam harvest festival in India and the Moon Festivals in Taiwan, where the incredible dragon boats of Taipei, Taiwan's capital, historically represented an appeal to the water gods to prevent disease, floods, and other disasters. It is believed this tradition has its roots in shamanistic rituals that began more than 3,000 years ago. Shamanism is a religion that involves a person with special healing qualities known as the shaman at its center. In ancient societies of northern Asia, beginning with hunter-gatherer cultures, this person, when in a state of ecstasy or trance, was believed to have the power to heal sickness and communicate with the world beyond. Drumming is thought to bring the shamans to this ecstasy, and drumming is always part of the dragon boat races during the Moon Festivals, as well as of many other harvest festivals throughout Asia.

Unique Customs and Traditions

Cows and the Coming Harvest in Cambodia

Cambodians celebrate their unique harvest with a festival known as Chrat Preah Nengkal during the month of May near the Royal Palace in Phnom Penh. During this observance, two members from the royal family go out to the fields and harness two cows in order to plough a small part of a field. After the ploughing is done, the cows are offered seven silver trays with rice, corn, wheat, beans, grass, water, and alcohol. The crowd waits in anticipation as the cows feed from the trays. Cambodians believe that if the cows eat the rice, corn, wheat, or beans, they will have a good coming harvest. However, if they eat the grass, the next harvest will not be good. If they choose to drink water, there will be a lot of rain (there might even be too much). If the alcohol lures them, the coming year might be filled with misfortune.

The Harvest Moon Festivals of China, Taiwan, and Vietnam

The full Moon is the central attraction in the autumn harvest festivals of East Asia. On the 15th day of the eighth month of the Chinese lunar calendar (which usually falls in September or October on the Gregorian calendar) the Moon is at its brightest for the entire year. On this day families

A child tastes a mooncake in a village in China during the Moon Festival.

and relatives come together to gaze at the Moon, have picnics near water, and hear the ancient stories that are part of the harvest Festival. Lantern-making and eating sweet pastries, called mooncakes, which are shaped like the full Moon, are the festival highlights for children and their families. In densely populated areas, the Moon Festivals may also include music, fireworks, and elaborate processions. In East Asia, it is also customary to tell the legend of the Moon goddess to children on this major holiday.

The Popularity of Tasty Moon Treats

Given the importance of rice in the cultures of Asia, nearly all of the Harvest Moon (mid-autumn) festivals on this vast continent celebrate with tasty moon-shaped treats that usually include rice flour. A world-renowned delight eaten during Harvest Moon Festivals is the mooncake. In some regions people exchange mooncakes as gifts. This is similar to the exchanging of fruitcakes among friends and relatives during the Christmas holiday season in the United States. There is an amazing variety of fillings inside the Moon pastries, including dates, fruit, sweet potato, nuts, chocolate, and even Chinese sausage. There are also green tea and coffee mooncakes.

In times past, mooncakes could take up to four weeks to make. However, the use of machines has helped to speed up the preparation. Today, in East Asia and throughout the Chinese diaspora, revelers celebrate with mooncakes at Moon Festivals.

Children make mooncakes at a kindergarten in China. Children make mooncakes to celebrate the Chinese Mid-Autumn Festival.

Mainstream Mooncakes

Even European and American companies such as Häagen-Dazs and Starbucks create mooncakes. As the Moon Festival has become more commercialized, more people are opting to buy mooncakes instead of make them, and mooncakes are frequently given as gifts by employers to employees. Mooncakes are sold in the early fall during the months leading up to the autumn harvest festivals, and not just in East Asia but also in many major cities around the world with large Asian populations, such as San Francisco.

Why Mooncakes Are Essential: Original Folk Tale of the Mooncake

The gift of a mooncake is believed by East Asians to bring good luck. These tasty full-Moon treats signify both completeness and harmony in the family and home. Along with the eating of mooncakes, the original folktale of the mooncake is often narrated during the harvest festival. In the 14th century, the Mongols controlled most of Central and East Asia and had established a dynasty in northern China, the Yuan dynasty. Chinese rebel leader Liu Fu Tong worked out a plan to rouse the Chinese people to rise up against the ruling Mongols. Liu Fu Tong told the Mongol leaders he wanted to give the gift of mooncakes to his friends in order to honor the Mongolian emperor. Little did the Mongols know, but Liu Fu Tong used the round mooncakes to hide information for his friends about the date that they would plan to revolt against the Mongols, encouraging his followers to rebel. Since the Mongols did not eat mooncakes, Liu Fu Tong knew this was a safe way to get the information to his people. The coup date was set for the 15th night of the eighth month of the Chinese lunar calendar. When his followers bit into the mooncakes, they discovered the revolutionary message, which led them to overthrow the Mongols and end the Yuan dynasty.

Harvest Festivals in India

Southern Indians celebrate their harvest festival called Pongal for four days in January. On the first day, this celebration is similar to their new year celebration, Diwali. To initiate the Pongal festival, they discard old clothes, and other used and worn objects are burned at a bonfire celebration. On the second day (Pongal day), Indians create their Pongal dish in the early morning. Made of rice, fresh milk, and unrefined sugar, the mixture is allowed to "boil over," which is what *pongal* means in Tamil, the language of many southern Indians. For this reason, Pongal is a symbol for abundance. People also prepare sweets, visit friends' and relatives' homes, and exchange greetings. The third day of Pongal honors cows and bullocks, sacred animals for Hindus of India. These cows and bullocks are fed the Pongal rice, milk, and sugar dish and then decorated and led in a procession to the beat of drums and music.

In the southwestern coastal state of Kerala, the harvest festival Onam is celebrated during the late summer. It is the most important annual observance in Kerala. In addition to the harvest, Onam celebrates an ancient king of Kerala named Mahabali, who was respected and loved because he took good care of his people. The people of Kerala believe that his spirit comes back to visit during the Onam celebrations.

With worship, music, dance, processions, and boat races, Onam celebrates a bountiful harvest following a year of hard work. Boat racing takes place on the Pampa River, where hundreds of men row boats adorned with red silk umbrellas draped with gold coins. The sight of the flashing, jingling boats is made even more dramatic with the sounds of the cymbal and drumbeats that fill the air during the race. The boats themselves are impressive in their shapes and styles, including the *chandan* boats, which are shaped like long snakes that slide gently and quickly through the Pampa River.

Like southern Indians preparing for Pongal, the people of Kerala prepare for Onam by cleaning their houses and decorating them. Women create stunning and complicated flower mats called *pookalam* in front of their homes to welcome the return of King Mahabali. Also, as they do at their Diwali New Year, the people of Kerala dress in beautiful new clothes purchased specifically for the Onam celebration. Of course, food is also central to this harvest festival. Delicious sweets, such as *payasam*, sweetened rice and milk pudding, and other favorite dishes are prepared and served on banana leaves for everyone's enjoyment.

A dancer attends celebrations to mark the start of the annual harvest festival of Onam in the southern Indian city of Kochi in 2007. The 10-day-long festival is celebrated annually in India's southern coastal state of Kerala to symbolize the return of King Mahabali.

A Shinto priest in Japan holds a wooden torch during the Tsukinami-sai ritual, one of the most important Shinto ceremonies held twice a year. It is a late-night-to-early-morning ritual to pray for a bumper harvest.

Workers and the Harvest Are Honored on the Same Day in Japan

On November 23, the people of Japan celebrate Labor Thanksgiving Day. Originally called the Shinto Harvest Festival, since 1948 all of Japan takes this day to honor the nation's workers as well as the result of the labor—the harvest. Traditionally the emperor would make the first offering of the fresh rice harvest to the gods on this day and then eat some himself. This ritual is still performed, but today it is a private ceremony. Labor Thanksgiving Day is a national holiday in Japan, so on this day, schools are closed. Other events often occur on this day, such as festivals that celebrate expanded worker and human rights since the end of World War II (1939–1945) in Japan.

Japan also celebrates Autumn Equinox Day, usually during September. It is a national holiday that marks the change of the seasons. Like Chusok in North and South Korea, it is a day when the Japanese show their respect

An archer on horseback aims at a target with an arrow during a *yabusame*, or horseback archery, performance at a Tokyo park in Japan. A total of 20 archers, dressed in traditional warrior's outfits, participate in the event. It was originally carried out as a prayer for peace and rich harvests by ancient warriors, who shot arrows at targets while riding at full gallop.

toward deceased relatives by going to their graves, cleaning their gravesites, praying to their ancestors, and offering them flowers, incense, and food. Celebrations may include *yabusame* events, a martial discipline with ancient origins in which riders on horseback shoot at targets.

The Naga Celebrate the Harvest in Myanmar

In mid-January in the northwest corner of Myanmar on the India-Myanmar border, the Naga people celebrate their new year, Kaing Bi. For the Naga, the new year festival is also the time to give thanks for their harvest. On New Year's Eve, which was recently permanently set

Minority Christians on the Subcontinent

While a majority of Myanmar is Buddhist and a majority of India is Hindu, the Naga tribes on the India-Myanmar border are mostly Christian. Some estimate that as many as 90 percent of the Naga on this border practice Christianity. This is the result of mostly Baptist missionaries from the West who converted the Naga during the middle of the 20th century. In recent years, there have been many claims that the Naga are persecuted in both India and Myanmar due to their Christian faith—sometimes, in Myanmar, being forced to renounce their beliefs.

A member of the Naga ethnic tribe, which lives in the northwest corner of Myanmar on the India-Myanmar border celebrates the Nagan new year, Kaing Bi, in mid-January. For the Naga, the new year festival is also a time to give thanks for their harvest.

at January 14, the new year festival pole is put up, and everyone gathers for the opening ceremony. A huge bonfire is lit to celebrate a good harvest, and everyone enjoys a traditional feast accompanied with rice wine.

The next day, hundreds of tourists, who have been invited to participate in the celebration and about 10,000 local people, gather to enjoy traditional Naga music and dancing along with traditional cooking and rice wine. The themes of the songs they sing deal with the importance of health, wealth, and happiness. There are also songs that express their hope for another good harvest in the coming year. The dancers come from each of the towns where the Naga live, and they wear costumes decorated with a hornbill's feathers, elephant tusks, buffalo horns, shells, and horses' tails. There are also dance contests between the different Naga villages, as well as other sporting events.

Chusok, a Harvest Moon Festival Is Celebrated by North and South Koreans

While North Korea is a communist state and divided from South Korea, both North and South Koreans still celebrate

A villager prays before floating a *krathong* into a pond during the Loy Krathong Festival in a town north of Bangkok, Thailand. Believers float *krathongs* during the festival, which is held as a symbolic apology to the goddess of the river.

their Harvest Moon Festival for two days in September. During this festival called Chusok, Koreans give thanks for a good harvest and begin the day by offering food and wine to their ancestors. These offerings are called *tshare*. Afterward, they visit their ancestors' graves at the cemetery. Chusok is also a day to attend family reunions, give and receive gifts, and participate in athletic events such as tug of war, archery contests, and wrestling matches.

During Chusok, Koreans prepare or buy a kind of rice mooncake cooked over pine needles called *shongpyun*. It is shaped like a half moon and is usually stuffed with beans, chestnuts, or sesame seeds with honey. Koreans eat these mooncakes during a traditional Chusok meal, along with fish, taro soup, mushrooms, and freshly picked fruit. Among the many activities during Chusok is an ancient dance performed in a circle by 10 to 20 women who sing traditional folk songs. Another dance called *talchum* involves traditional songs and masks, as well as a drama where the masked characters represent people, animals, or mystical creatures.

Water and Fire for Moon Festival in Thailand

Thailand celebrates a full Moon Festival called Loy Krathong around November of every year. *Loy* means "to float" and *krathong* is a boat made of banana leaves. On the night of the full Moon, people put candles in their *krathong* and send them out onto bodies of water (rivers, ponds, or canals). Thais believe that these *krathongs* can take away their sins as well as misfortune. Along with this custom, the Thai people also celebrate with fireworks and beauty pageants.

Europe

Europe is the second-smallest continent on Earth by size, yet it is the third largest by population with 731 million inhabitants. Bounded by the Ural Mountains on the east, the Atlantic Ocean on the west, the Mediterranean Sea on the south and the Arctic Ocean on the north, its 3.9 million square miles are home to diverse agricultural traditions. The Gulf Stream, a strong current of warm water that flows across the Atlantic Ocean, helps to maintain a fairly mild temperature throughout the continent. It does this largely by warming the winds that blow off the ocean and by bringing significant moisture to both the coastlines and the mainland.

People gather around the traditional St. John the Baptist bonfire marking the summer solstice in Germany.

Young Belarusian girls put flower wreaths in water during the ancient Slavic pagan Midsummer Night Festival in Belarus.

Midsummer's Day by Another Name Is St. John

While Midsummer celebrations in Europe differ from country to country—and may be known as St. John's Day, Midsummer's Day, or Midsummer's Eve—most involve large bonfires in the countryside, a tradition that has carried over from ancient times. In France, Portugal, Denmark, Germany, Ireland, Italy, Latvia, Finland, Sweden, Norway, and Estonia, the fires are usually lit at midnight and stay alive throughout the night while people dance and sing around them.

St. Martin's Day in Northern Europe

Today St. Martin's Day is observed by northern Europeans as a harvest festival marking the beginning of winter and the end of the fiscal (financial) year. But the day originally commemorated the birth of St. Martin (the Catholic patron saint of France) in the fourth century. According to the tale, when the people first wanted St. Martin as their bishop, he was not interested and tried to escape the crowds by hiding among the geese. However, the geese gave him away by gabbling. For that reason, today people eat geese as part of the traditional meal for the Feast of St. Martin on November 11— to punish them for their betrayal.

In many northern European countries such as Denmark and the Netherlands, a famous story about St. Martin's generosity is reenacted on St. Martin's Day. According to the story, on a frigid winter day in France Martin noticed a beggar nearby who appeared to be freezing. Martin took off his own warm cloak and, with his sword, sliced it in two equal pieces. He gave half to the beggar. The following evening, Martin had a dream that he had given half of his cloak to Jesus. When people celebrate St. Martin's Day in some parts of Europe, they hold a parade with a person representing St. Martin on a horse and sometimes with the beggar that he saved from the cold as well.

Celebrating Sukkot in Europe

Jewish Europeans, especially in France, the United Kingdom, and Russia, where more than 1 million European Jews live, celebrate the Sukkot autumn thanksgiving. The Hebrew Bible refers to the Feast of the Ingathering in the book of Exodus, marking the end of the harvest, and Leviticus describes the period when the Israelites lived in huts (sukkah) while wandering in the wilderness after the Exodus from Egypt. Because of these references, over a seven-day period, Jews erect huts made of branches and honor God with prayers of thanksgiving for the fertility of the land, and they thank God for

Before Homeopathy, It Was Still Medicine

Ancient people believed that St.-John's-wort, a shrubby plant with yellow flowers and oval petals, could rid them of evil spirits. In ancient Greece it was used to treat various ailments (such as nervous disorders and bites from poisonous reptiles) and today it is sometimes prescribed to help with burns, bacterial infections, and to relieve depression. Many people in the United States buy this herbal remedy over the counter, but scientific studies differ on how well it works on a variety of illnesses and disorders. It also reacts badly at times with other medications and doctors caution patients about these interactions before suggesting this popular herbal supplement.

watching over them during the 40 long years that their ancestors were without permanent homes. Jewish families also dine in the sukkah to re-create the feeling of being without a permanent home, in connection to their ancestors.

European Jews celebrate Sukkot in the same way as celebrants do all over the world. For Reform Jews and in Israel, the ceremony lasts for seven days. Dinner under the stars in sukkahs, however, might be a little colder in northern Europe in the fall than they are in Israel. For Orthodox Jews, it is an eight-day observance.

Unique Customs and Traditions

Midsummer in Andorra

In the tiny, mountainous country of Andorra, located between France and Spain in southwestern Europe, a town elder prays for a good harvest and then lights the bonfire. Then the crowd moves clockwise around the fire, while praying and throwing broken items, rosary beads, and religious statues into the flames. On this night, men light torches from the bonfire and walk across their fields in hope that the fields will be spared from damage. When the fire is out, the ashes are sprinkled on four corners of the fields to bless the harvest.

St. Leopold's Day in Austria

In Austria St. Leopold's Day is a harvest festival that celebrates St. Leopold, an 11th-century Austrian saint known for his devoutness and good works. Additionally, the day celebrates Leopoldsberg wine, made by monks in Klosterneuberg Abbey (founded by St. Leopold), and many of the traditions associated with this celebration

Women in traditional clothes bring baskets with fruits and vegetables during a St. Leopold's ceremony in a town in Austria.

involve games and tributes to the wine. One tradition on St. Leopold's Day that requires a bit of athleticism is called *Fasselrutschen*. First, participants, including young and old alike, climb up a giant 12,000-gallon, 300-year-old barrel of wine and then slide down the side of it for luck. It is believed that the more treacherous the ride, the greater the slider's luck will be.

St. Martin's Day in Denmark

For Danes St. Martin's Day is a time to settle old debts. Since it occurs when winter begins, many pagan traditions are connected with this holiday, such as the Martin's Fire, which is a celebration with bonfires or burning wheels. During the evening of St. Martin's Day, children carry Martin's lanterns, parade through the streets, and sing about the generosity of the saint. Children also go from house to house and recite verses, for which they are given sweets or sometimes even money.

Some celebrants also take part in a tradition involving burning a straw witch in the bonfires. This tradition probably came about as a reminder of the 16th century witch burnings that occurred throughout the Western world. The witch represents a community's collective worries—and the burning sends witches away to Bloksbjerg, a mountain in Germany (called Blocksberg in German) where a great witch gathering was thought to be held on this day.

Jaanipäev in Estonia

In the northeastern European county of Estonia, Midsummer's Day is known as Jaanipäev, which marks the end of sowing and the beginning

A Night to Remember

In Estonian fairy tales, two lovers, Koit (dawn) and Hämarik (dusk), see each other only once a year on Midsummer's Eve to exchange just one tender kiss. This night is believed to be an important one for couples.

of hay-making. It also serves as an independence day because it comes right after an important date in Estonian history. On Midsummer night, a huge bonfire is lit at midnight, around which people dance and sing and play games. In pre-Christian times, people believed that during the darkest part of the night, good and evil come together, and flames have a purifying effect that wards off evil. In present times, Estonians will also light smaller bonfires to jump over, which is believed to ensure good luck for the coming harvest.

Midsummer in Estonia comes right after Victory Day, which celebrates Estonia's triumph over Baltic-German armed forces to regain Estonia's independence on June 23, 1919. On this day, the president of Estonia lights a victory flame that is then taken around to bonfires all over the country. In this way, Estonian pride and nationalism are tied directly to their most important harvest celebration. Jaanipäev became a national holiday in 1992.

Juhannasaatto and Flag Day in Finland

In Finland Midsummer's Day, or Juhannasaatto, is an official holiday and schools and businesses are closed. People dress in traditional Finnish costume (shirts, vests, and skirts for women; shirts, long trousers, and knee breeches for men, all made of wool and dyed with colors derived from nature), and the huge bonfires sometimes require a ticket to attend. Families and friends get together for picnics in the countryside and share popular dishes such as pickled or smoked fish, potatoes, and the very first strawberries of the season (often served with beer). Towns and cities empty out on Juhannasaatto, as celebrations take place in the countryside and along the coast. Also, since Juhannasaatto coincides with Finnish Flag Day, the white and blue Finnish flag flies proudly through the night, illuminated by the bonfires.

O'zapft Is! Oktoberfest in Germany

The ceremonial cry of *O'zapft is!* during Oktoberfest means "The keg has been tapped!" This leaves little doubt that beer plays a major role in the

An overview shows one of the huge beer tents at Oktoberfest, the biggest beer festival in the world, in Munich, Germany. For 18 days locals and tourists gather to consume millions of gallons of beer and hundreds of thousands of sausages.

German harvest festival. Perhaps the most famous alcohol-related harvest festival of all, Oktoberfest originated with the royal wedding of King Ludwig I of Bavaria (located in southern Germany) and Queen Therese von Sachsen-Hildburghausen (also of Bavaria) on October 12, 1810. The wedding celebrations included a bountiful beer party and horse racing for the people.

Since this first party in 1810, Munich (the capital of Bavaria) has hosted the communal beer parties in large tents. The customary festival opening takes place in September with the arrival of the mayor of Munich in a festive coach, followed by a horse-drawn brewer's cart. A big parade follows, and at the end of the procession the mayor taps the first keg with the cry of *O'zapft is!* Tourists from other parts of Germany and around the world and Bavarians wearing traditional costumes such as lederhosen (leather knee-breeches) and leather suspenders, celebrate for hours on end. The most famous beer festival in the world, das *Bierfest* (which means "the beerfest"), occurs during Oktoberfest. Besides drinking a lot of beer, the festival also includes amusement park rides, circuses, food courts, carnival booths, and live bands playing a wide variety of music. Today Oktoberfest is celebrated all over the world wherever Germans have settled—from its original home of Munich, Germany, to Windhoek, the capital of Namibia, to the resort town of Big Bear in the mountains of Southern California.

Midsummer in Norway

People in Norway believed that lighting midnight fires banished sickness from cattle and from people who worked the land. In a belief related to Denmark's, the large bonfires are thought to keep off the witches who are

---

A Scandinavian Midsummer Song

We shall not sleep away the summer night;
She is too light for that.
Then shall we wander together out
Under the leaf-heavy trees,
Under the leaf-heavy trees.

We shall not sleep away from the hay-sown field
And the grasshopper's play in the meadow,
But wander together under
Pale blue heavens
'Til the birds lift their wings.
'Til the birds lift their wings.

And feel that we are kin with the earth,
With the wind and white clouds,
And know that we shall be together
Until the morning's dawn.
Until the morning's dawn.

— "Vi Skal Ikkje Sova Burt Sumarnatta," composed by Geirr Tveitt from a poem by Aslaug Låstad Lygre

---

The Midsummer pole, which is like a maypole, is raised during Midsummer celebrations in the Swedish town of Leksand, northwest of Stockholm. The annual event in Leksand is the largest midsummer festival in Sweden.

flying from all parts that night into the German Blocksberg Mountain where the "big witch" lives.

Midsummer in Sweden

In Sweden (and the Swedish-speaking coastal areas of Finland), Midsummer celebrations do not include bonfires. In their place are Midsummer poles, similar to maypoles (tall flower-wreathed poles), which Swedes dance around while people sing and play games. In ancient times, this pole represented fertility and symbolized the impregnating of Mother Earth. Swedes also dine on traditional dishes of pickled herring, sour cream, potatoes, and strawberries on this day, and porches all over the country are decorated with birches and leafy branches.

The Midsummer night, the shortest of the year, was thought to be a magical time when plants and the dewdrops on them possessed healing powers. During this night in Sweden, people would go into the woods to pick and gather plants and herbs that were believed to have healing powers, such as St.-John's-wort. One Swedish tradition holds that if a young woman sleeps on wildflowers she has gathered, she will dream of her future mate on this night of the year. Today, many people decorate their porches with silver birches, lilacs, and other branches that they collect or

Two young women with flower garlands in their hair, pick bouquets of wildflowers in preparation for the annual Midsummer holidays. Swedes traditionally celebrate Midsummer with dancing and feasting, and unmarried young women sleep on wildflowers to dream of their loved ones during the shortest night of the year.

buy to celebrate the harvest. Wreathes liven up doors, and flower crowns adorn the heads of young women on Midsummer's day. Many wear the colorful traditional dress of their country—skirts, bodices, and hats for women, and waistcoats, breeches, and leggings for men.

Latin America and the Caribbean

Latin America is the name given to the region of the Americas where languages derived from Latin—Spanish, French, and Portuguese—are spoken. This includes the bulk of Central and South America as well as certain islands in the Caribbean. Geographically, Latin America is bounded by the Atlantic Ocean to the east and the Pacific Ocean to the west. It is home to the largest river in the world, the Amazon, and the longest mountain range, the Andes. The Latin American region has a wide array of climates, from extremely dry deserts to lush rain forests, but the majority of it is temperate to warm with adequate rainfall. These factors have made for a rich agricultural tradition, with evidence of subsistence farming dating as far back as 6500 B.C.E.

Honoring Pachamama

In many South American countries, the beginning of August brings various Pachamama harvest festivals. Pachamama is a goddess worshipped by peoples of the Andes Mountains. She is the protector of planting and harvesting. In the same way that many harvest festivals worldwide have been linked to St. John, the Catholic Church in Latin America attempted to tie the pre-Incan Earth goddess Pachamama to the Virgin Mary. While in many areas they were successful, Pachamama is also still worshipped and celebrated regionally as the main focus of some South American harvest festivals, often alongside Catholic saints. There are both family ceremonies and community-wide rituals in her honor. In

A man places a gift of coca leaves on an altar in the Andes Mountains where Bolivians leave gifts for Pachamama (Mother Earth). People leave offerings of flowers, alcohol, and coca leaves to deities, as a way to give thanks and ask for favors.

one ritual, villagers gather around a pit that has been marked with stones. In the pit, they place items traditionally offered to the goddess: corn flour and grains of corn, cooked food, and *chicha*, a corn beer still popular today. Each aspect of this ritual emphasizes one facet of the goddess's three-part identity. The rocks that will cover the pit represent Pachamama of the sky: Janaj Pacha. The offerings themselves are symbolic of Pachamama of the soil: Kay Pacha. Finally, the pit itself honors Pachamama of the underworld: Ukhu Pacha.

It is important that both a woman and a man take part in the ceremonies honoring the union of Pachamama and her husband, the Sun god Inti, who were both benevolent deities. One origin myth tells of how Inti led a brother and sister named Manco Capak and Mama Ocllo off an island in the center of Lake Titicaca (located between Bolivia and Peru). He gave them a golden stick that would test the land to see if it was suitable for cultivation. The two eventually used the stick to find the location in which to establish the Inca civilization.

Indigenous Bolivians carry bundles of corn crops while they dance during the traditional Harvest Festival in Bolivia. This traditional dance is to thank the Pachamama, or Mother Earth, for her good crops.

Colonial-Era Harvest Festivals: European and African Traditions

Some harvest festivals date from colonial times and are more influenced by European and African traditions than indigenous ones. This is especially true for crops that were widely introduced when parts of Latin America and the Caribbean were under European control. During this period, the Europeans planted entire regions of Latin America and the Caribbean, such as southern Mexico and Haiti, with one crop, creating what is called a mono-crop culture. Such was the case with sugarcane. By the middle of the 18th century, the Caribbean was a large producer of sugar throughout the world, fueled in part by the slave trade that brought numerous Africans to do the hard labor in the fields. In the 1780s, Barbados was the largest producer of sugarcane in the world. Due to the numbers of Africans involved in harvesting sugar, African influences played and continue to play a role in the thanksgiving festivals associated with sugarcane.

Wine Festivals in South America: Blessing the Grapes

Grapes are another important colonial-era crop that has major commercial importance for certain regions, especially in South America. They were first brought to Latin America, along with wheat, by Spanish Jesuit missionaries for use in Catholic communion rites. The fertile areas of Chile, Peru, and Argentina were discovered to be ideal for growing wine. Today Argentina is the largest producer of wine in the Southern Hemisphere and Peru's wine industry is growing and gaining recognition. The Ica region in Peru and the Mendoza region of Argentina both hold wine harvest festivals every March during the grape season. These festivals are known as El Festival de la Vendimia, often simply called Vendimia.

Unique Customs and Traditions

Burnt Offerings for the Earth Goddess in Argentina

In northern Argentina, the people of the Puna (a high-altitude region of the Andes Mountains characterized by plateaus and cliffs) celebrate

The Flowing Music of the Andes

Traditional Andean music can be heard all over the world today, played by street musicians or during European street fairs and in North American cities. Contemporary musical arrangements in the cities and in the Andean countryside usually include the 10-stringed *charango*, which is based on the guitars that the Spanish brought to the New World. In the 1960s, musicians Simon and Garfunkel helped to popularize the Andean song *El Cóndor Pasa* when they used the melody in their widely popular song by the same name (but with different lyrics). Today it is probably the best-known South American melody in the Western world.

the Festival to Pachamama, continuing ancient rites to give thanks to Mother Earth for the corn harvest. People drink *chicha*, dance, and play the ancient instruments of the Andes, including *quenas* (flutes) and *sikus* (panpipes). Families collect house trash from the four corners of the home and burn it with aromatic herbs from the mountains. The burned items are then buried in a deep hole dug in the family yard or on top of a hill, along with coca leaves, cigarettes, and other offerings—such as cooked food in a clay pot, or even a llama fetus. *Chicha* is then poured over the hole. The belief is that Pachamama might need these things throughout the coming year.

A family or community will often pray together, apologizing for having to take so much from the Earth, and giving thanks to Pachamama for the year's harvest. The Festival to Pachamama will continue throughout the month of August with the dissonant music of the *siku* and *quenas* often playing for hours on end and sometimes all night long.

Crowning the Grape Harvest Queen in Argentina

In Argentina, the wine festival begins when the clergy blesses the grapes on the vine, and in Mendoza, Argentina, as in Peru, choosing the wine festival beauty queen is a major part of the celebration. In Mendoza, the contestants from each region ride on elaborate floats in parades that take

A 14-year-old Argentinian girl lugs crates of freshly harvested grapes from the fields to waiting farm trucks. Argentina, the largest producer of wine in the Southern Hemisphere, celebrates the grape harvest each year with a wine festival.

place Friday and Saturday in the down-town area. Saturday night the Harvest Queen is chosen during a glitzy specta-cle that includes music, light shows, and dancing. Thousands watch the crowning of the new queen and listen to speeches made by former queens.

St. John's Day in Aruba

As has occurred in many countries of Europe, harvest festivals renamed for saints now take place in parts of Latin America. In Aruba, a tiny Caribbean island just north of Venezuela, June 24 is St. John's Day. St. John's Day is also known as Dera Gai, meaning "burying the rooster," which is symbolic of a successful harvest. Dera Gai came to Aruba by way

Traditional Grape Juice Extraction

The ancient process of grape stomping helped to break open the grapes and push out their juice without harming the grape stem too much. If the stem is damaged, it can release a bitter flavor that harms the wine's taste. Feet were used because they were gentle on the grapes and padded, which helped to protect the feet and push out the juice. Grape stomping, though squishy and fun to do in small tubs during harvest festivals today, is very tiring work. In fact, it takes around 100 pounds of grapes to make just seven gal-lons of wine Not surprisingly, most large-scale wine makers use machines now to extract the sweet grape juices.

A Venezuelan couple dances to the rhythm of the drums as they celebrate the Dia de San Juan (St. John's Day), a festival that draws on European and African roots in a village in northern Venezuela. The festival starts when the saint is brought out from the church and ends after three days of non-stop drumming, singing, dancing, and drinking.

of ancient Mexico and South America, and was originally a harvest festival, possibly of Arawak origins, to give thanks to many gods for the year's crops. The Arawak are believed to be the first native people in what is now Latin America, and the first people seen by Christopher Columbus when he set foot in the Americas. Catholic priests combined this celebration with the traditional Dia de San Juan (St. John's Day), in an effort to convert the people of Aruba to Christianity.

One of the main events of Dera Gai in Aruba is a game that begins with burying a rubber chicken, representing a rooster, up to its neck in the sand. A gourd is then placed over the head of the "rooster." People take turns being blindfolded and trying to hit the gourd with a stick while everyone dances and sings in a circle around him. They sing:

San Juan ta bin, San Juan ta bai
Ate cu e palo den su man
[Saint John comes, Saint John goes
There he is with the stick in his hand]

The person who successfully hits the rooster wins it. Earlier Dera Gai festivals used live roosters that were then sacrificed and eaten on this day.

Another early tradition of Dera Gai involved, and in some places still involves, the burning of the leftover crops at the end of the festival, which Arubans believe purifies the soul. Because of this belief, the men and women of Aruba wear bright red and yellow outfits on St. John's Day to symbolize fire.

The Blessings of St. John's Day

There are many other St. John's Day celebrations around the world that are not exclusively harvest festivals. In Puerto Rico, St. John's Day actually begins on St. John's Night, or Noche de San Juan. On this night at midnight, it is believed that all water is blessed with extraordinary powers and can increase fertility, agricultural production, and beauty, as well as improve one's fortune. In Puerto Rico, people often walk backward toward the beach and sometimes even do back flips in the water at the stroke of midnight. The belief is that this will bring good luck and keep away evil for the next year. Several days leading up to this special night are also full of excitement, with events such as boxing, karate exhibitions, rock bands, and salsa dancing.

Calypso Rules at Kadooment in the Bahamas and in Barbados

On August 2 in the capital city of Nassau in the Bahamas, and during the end of July and beginning of August in Barbados, throngs of people celebrate Kadooment, which is also known as Crop Over. This melodic harvest festival begins with the delivery of the last sugarcanes, indicating that the year's crop harvest is over. At this time, a ceremony is held to mark the official end of the cane harvesting season and to crown the most productive cane cutters as king and queen of the Crop Over festival.

Revelers with painted bodies dance during the Kadooment Parade in Barbados.

Revelers dance during the Kadooment Parade in Barbados. The Kadooment Day Parade is an annual harvest festival event in Barbados, when thousands of participants take to the streets wearing costumes and dancing to calypso music.

In both island countries, dancing in the streets and calypso music are central to the celebrations, as are vibrantly dressed musicians in Kadooment and Tuk bands who play tin flutes and kettledrums. In Barbados, bands compete for the coveted Calypso Monarch Award, given to the best calypso band of the year. The celebration lasts five days in Barbados and the most important day, Kadooment Day, is a public holiday. Another part of the Barbados celebration is a very competitive costume contest in which each participant hopes to be named Designer of the Year. Following a massive procession that moves from the National Stadium to the Spring Garden, there is a huge, raucous party that continues late into the night with drinking, dancing, eating, and fireworks. Many celebrants choose to end the festivities with a group swim at a nearby beach.

Homespun Island Music

Calypso is a type of folk music popularized in the early 19th century. The songs are usually about local politics and include other social commentary. They are sung using a mixture of Spanish, Creole, and African phrases. The instruments that accompany the songs are a kind of maraca called the *shak-shak*, a small Latin American guitar called the *cuatro*, and bamboo poles that are struck on the ground. Steel bands made up of oil-drum orchestras also provide accompaniment.

The Vast Andes Mountain Range

The Andes are enormous mountains in South America that include some of the world's tallest peaks. They are also the longest range of mountains on Earth, extending 5,500 miles from the Caribbean coast in the north to Tierra del Fuego, an archipelago (or chain of islands) in southern Argentina and Chile. The Andean countries of South America include Colombia, Ecuador, Peru, Bolivia, and Chile.

Worshipping the Earth Mother in Bolivia

In Bolivia, Aymara Indians, whose ancestry pre-dates the Inca, make offerings throughout the year to Pachamama in order to ensure good harvests and good fortune for a home or community. Though her name is commonly translated as "Earth Mother," Pacha refers not only to the Earth but also to the universe and to all of time.

A family might burn and bury an array of items under their home, such as an offering of *chicha* beer or sugar tablets with symbols on them representing the family's hopes—a condor for good luck and peace, a house for shelter, or a picture of a mountain for successful travel. Offerings to Pachamama lie buried under most Bolivian homes. These are gifts to the Earth Mother, a way of apologizing for asking so much of her every year.

Yam Festivals in Haiti and Jamaica

Yams have been grown and eaten in the Caribbean since they found their way onto the slave ships coming from West Africa to the Caribbean during the 18th century. As in West Africa, in Haiti and Jamaica yams are an important local crop grown for local consumption and also cultivated for sale. While yams are far more important as an export crop in Africa, they are still celebrated in the Caribbean during two distinct festivals.

On November 25, rural Haitians celebrate the Mangé Yam Festival. For the celebration, farmers decorate their carts and paint the horns of their bulls. As in Africa, yams are given as offerings to ancestors and to the local gods so that the next crop will produce plenty for all. In Jamaica the South Trelawny Yam Festival is celebrated in the town of Falmouth. The yellow yam from South Trelawny is renowned as one of the best in the world. Beginning in 1997, Trelawny residents established this festival as a way to attract tourists and to educate the country about this region's scrumptious yams. Celebrated in April every year, the Trelawny Yam Festival features song, poetry, and dance festivals, educational events that highlight the history and culture of the yam farmer, half marathons, a beauty pageant, and bike races. It also features and sells the versatile yam cooked and configured into a multitude of dishes including yam wine, yam porridge, and even yam ice cream. One main attraction is the Yam Culinary Area where visitors can watch professional chefs prepare yam dishes and demonstrate yam carving.

Food, Music, Dancing, and Wine in Peru

As in Mendoza, Argentina, in Ica, Peru a major part of the festival involves tasting wine from the many vineyards in the region. There is also a large variety of music such as rock, reggaetón, salsa, cumbia, and latino oldies. In Peru, everyone dances to the Afro-Peruvian music that characterizes this region. People also devour local sweets known as *tejas*, made from pecans or candied fruits, filled with caramel (similar to the Spanish delicacy *dulce de leche*) and covered with a sugar shell. For chocolate lovers, there is a chocolate version, known as a *chocoteja*. Some festival visitors enjoy eating *tejas* while drinking *pisco*, an aromatic grape brandy that originated in this part of southern Peru four centuries ago.

Another Peruvian festival that celebrates the harvest is Inti Raymi, an Incan ceremony that was harshly suppressed under the Spanish

A man dressed as the Inca Sun god waves from a dais in Inti Raymi, an Inca ceremony of thanks in Cuzco, Peru. The Sun, the main god of the Inca civilization, was considered the creator of all that existed and presided over the destiny of human beings and of the universe.

for centuries but has returned, much to the delight of local Peruvians and the thousands that visit Peru in the summer. The Inti Raymi festival honors the most important Incan god, the Sun god. In pre-Columbian time, it occurred during the summer solstice when the Sun was farthest from the Earth, around the end of June. For the Inca, this crucial ceremony was their way of pleading with their god to return so that the harvest would be bountiful. Revived in 1944, today the ceremony is celebrated by thousands every summer in Cuzco, Peru, and honors the Sun god and his marriage to the Inca. Whereas in Incan times it spanned three days and included animal sacrifices, fasting, and feasting, since its reintroduction the festival has grown into a week-long celebration second only in popularity to Brazil's Carnival in Rio de Janeiro.

During this week, revelers participate in parades, music, and dancing. People wear large amounts of gold and silver to honor their Incan ancestors and the Sun god. A major element of Inti Raymi, enjoyed by participants and thousands of Cuzco tourists, is a procession led by ceremonial virgins who wind through the streets to the Sacayhuaman fortress ruins in the hills above Cuzco. Sacayhuaman is also known as the House of the Sun. There, speeches honoring the Sun and the Peruvians' Inca past are delivered in Quechua, the language of the Inca. Originally a white llama would be slaughtered and its remains examined to discover what would happen during the coming year. Now, a realistic stage act takes the place of an actual sacrifice.

The Inca developed sophisticated animal husbandry systems to domesticate and breed the llama for strength and endurance. The llamas were highly respected animals until the arrival of the Spanish. When the

A llama overlooks the Incan ruins at Machu Picchu, Peru. The llama is a New World relative of the camel, native to the Puna region of the Andes. This animal was extremely important to the Inca and other Andean indigenous groups.

The Valuable Llama

The llama is a New World relative of the camel, native to the Puna region of the Andes Mountains. This animal was an extremely important part of daily life for the Inca and other Andean indigenous groups. As pack animals, they could not only navigate the difficult terrain of the high altitudes, but they were also a source of food and clothing for the Inca. Just as the American Indians depended on the buffalo, the indigenous people of South America depended on the llama and its three New World relatives: the alpaca, the guanaco, and the vicuña.

Spanish conquered the Inca, the llama was replaced by domesticated European animals, and many llamas were killed off. However, llamas are still widely used by the poor in the extremely high altitudes of the Puna region, since other animals do not adapt well to such difficult conditions. Today, while no longer as central in importance because of modern technology, the llama and its relatives are regaining popularity and protection through national preservation efforts.

Middle East

The regions that make up the Middle East include plains and mountains, the very deep Dead Sea (this salty water mass is the lowest point on Earth's surface), and abundant flowing rivers. This area of the world is where agriculture was born and along with it, the earliest identified civilization, some 8,000 years ago, in an area now called the Fertile Crescent. This curved region between the Arabian Desert and the Armenian mountains extends between Egypt and the Persian Gulf and probably had a lusher climate than it does today.

Giving Thanks to God and the Many Gods that Deliver the Goods

Harvest festivals in the Middle East are colorful, musical, and tasty events, some taking place at the beginning of the harvest and others at the end to celebrate the fruitfulness of the land and to thank God or the gods for blessing the land. With kite flying in Afghanistan, dancing and singing in Egypt, and the building of ancient farmer's huts in Israel, harvest festival activities are always family affairs. They also recognize the importance of God's (or the gods') role in fertilizing the Earth and providing for its people. This is especially important for cultures in the Middle East, one of the driest regions on Earth.

Food in a Dry Place

The majority of the regions in the Middle East share the common characteristic of being extremely dry, most not receiving more than 12 inches of rain a year. Deserts are the major land formation; the Middle East includes parts of the Sahara, the Arabian Desert, and the Negev. Today much of the Middle East's food supply must be imported from other areas in order to meet the basic food needs of its people. While oil is certainly an important resource for many Middle Eastern countries, the resource on many Middle Eastern minds is water and how to get enough of it in order to survive.

Religious Associations, Outdoor Picnics, and Family Gatherings

Some Middle Eastern countries have harvest festivals in the spring to celebrate the beginning of the harvest season. While many of these festivals have pagan roots, today many are at least nominally tied to Islam and Christianity, two of the monotheistic religions that were born in the Middle East. One harvest festival in Egypt, Sham el Nessim, is now directly after Coptic Easter and today it is celebrated by Egyptian Christians and Muslims alike. (Coptic Christians are a branch of Eastern Orthodox Christians common in Egypt.) Both Egyptians and Afghans celebrate their harvests with outdoor family picnics.

Jews in Israel celebrate the harvest festival Sukkot in the fall, and this observance also takes place largely out of doors. As in Egypt and Afghanistan, family plays a central role in the festival activities. However, unlike many other harvest celebrations, the central customs and rites of Sukkot are directly tied to Judaism and not to pagan traditions. Judaism is the religion practiced by nearly 80 percent of all Israelis and is the oldest of the three major monotheistic religions, beginning almost 4,000 years ago.

Unique Customs and Traditions
Sham el Nessim in Egypt

One of the most popular festivals in Egypt is known as Sham el Nessim, which literally means "sniffing the breeze." Sham el Nessim has been celebrated for more than 4,500 years. Its name is derived from the ancient Egyptian word for the harvest season, *Shamo*. In the springtime, ancient Egyptians would give thanks to their deities for a bountiful Shamo by offering foods such as fish and onions. Over many thousands of years and the dawning of Christianity the holiday developed into its current form: a nationwide celebration that looks back on the productivity of the past year and ahead to the aspirations of the next. On the first Monday following the Coptic Easter, families will venture out of the city centers into nature to partake in a traditional picnic of salt fish, green onions, and lettuce, among other things. The entire day is spent outdoors, "smelling the breeze" and anticipating the coming of a new planting cycle. In some larger parks there may be dance concerts or storytellers throughout the day; other festivities include parades, marching bands, and garden tours.

Sukkot, a Time of Joy and Thanksgiving in Israel

When you harvest your crops from your granary and your vineyard,
you should be happy on your holiday, you and your children...
                                    —Deuteronomy 16:13

In Israel during the High Holy Days, solemn and sacred rites and rituals are performed to observe Rosh Hashanah and to prepare for the new year to come, including the celebration of the harvest festival Sukkot. The name of the festival comes from the word *sukkah*, or "booth," a temporary structure in which ancient Israelites found sanctuary. In the five days between Yom Kippur (a Jewish holiday that follows Rosh Hashanah) and Sukkot in Israel, Jewish families as well as businesses erect the sukkah—which are similar to the booths or huts where Israelites resided for 40 years in the desert. There are four plants required for the sukkah: palm fronds, citron, myrtle sprigs, and willow branches, all of which are blessed in a festive prayer. According to Jewish Holy Books, the sukkah must have at least three walls and can be made of many kinds of material. The roof is a temporary one, made of branches of trees or anything that comes from the ground, and must be open enough so that the stars and sky peek through. Some kosher restaurants around Jerusalem build elaborate sukkahs and offer holiday specials to attract customers. Even the Israeli army bases have erected sukkahs.

In Israel, it is possible to see sukkahs all over towns and cities; they are constructed in parking lots, on balconies and rooftops, and on lawns. Families will put all sorts of decorations on the sukkah to make it welcoming and pleasing, especially ones representing the first fruits, such as gourds, or Rosh Hashanah cards. When built, the Holy

Orthodox Jews in Jerusalem buy palm branches to place on the roof of the sukkah, a temporary booth, built for the holiday Sukkot. Religious Jews eat, sleep, and study in the sukkah during the seven-day holiday that remembers the Israelites' wanderings for 40 years in the desert after leaving Egypt.

Welcome at the Sukkah

According to Jewish mystics, the biblical figures Abraham, Isaac, Jacob, Moses, Aaron, Joseph, and David show up on the seven nights of Sukkot to visit every sukkah and serve as a symbolic guest. During Sukkot, Jews are also encouraged to welcome in those who do not have their own sukkah in which to celebrate.

Books command that Jews dwell in these huts. Most fulfill this commandment by eating meals in the sukkah for the seven days. When possible and weather permitting, some Jews also spend all day and even the night in these temporary homes as a way of experiencing what their ancestors experienced. On the seventh day of Sukkot, called Hoshana Rabbah, celebrants recite the words "help us, we pray" (hosanna) over and

Sleep, but not Too Much

Jews used to celebrate the harvest in the spring as well. As fewer and fewer people over the centuries directly worked the land, the spring harvest festival was transformed into a holiday called Shavuot. On Shavuot, which falls on the third month of the Jewish calendar and 50 days after Passover (the day when Jews celebrate the release of the Israelites from slavery in Egypt) Jews commemorate God giving the Ten Commandments to Moses on Mount Sinai. According to Jewish parables, the Israelites actually overslept on the morning of God's visit. To compensate for this negligence, Jews hold a vigil on the eve of Shavuot. They stay awake from dusk to dawn, keeping themselves busy with readings from their Holy Books. Another Shavuot custom is eating dairy foods. One explanation for this comes from a passage in the Torah: "And He gave us this land, a land flowing with milk and honey." (Deut. 26:9) Some Jews also adorn their houses with flowers and other greenery as a reminder of the original agricultural significance of the holiday.

An Orthodox Jewish man walks past sukkahs, in Jerusalem.

over while carrying bundles of twigs from willow trees as they circle the synagogue seven times. This practice is related to the belief that God decides the amount of rainfall to be sent down on the Earth to ensure good coming harvests.

In Israel, businesses are closed on the first and the last days of Sukkot. The days in between are considered semi-holy days, which means that many businesses are only open half days. Families travel to vacation spots during this time and take part in other festivals. For example, during Sukkot Israelis might attend a jewelry show in Jerusalem, or wine fests and comedy festivals in Beersheba, the largest city in southern Israel's Negev Desert. They may also attend an Israeli cowboy festival, and even reggae shows at major amphitheaters throughout Israel.

The end of Sukkot marks the start of the rainy season. In Israel, the day immediately after Sukkot is called Sh'mini Atzeret. Since ancient times, Jews have been instructed to pray to God on this day for plentiful rain to sustain them through the winter.

North America

Across the sprawling land mass of North America, survival has always been a cause for celebration. The customary harvest observances in both the United States and Canada are called Thanksgiving. For Canadians,

Giant balloons are a favorite feature of the annual Macy's Thanksgiving Day Parade in New York City.

the unofficial celebrations of the holiday date back to 1578 when explorer Martin Frobisher held a feast to celebrate his band's survival of a quest to discover a hidden northern route to Asian countries. It was believed for centuries that the right navigator could succeed in finding a trade passage through Canada's inland sea, the Hudson Bay. Canada made the celebration a state holiday in 1872. For modern generations, it has been a time of family gathering and feasting and falls on the Monday closest to Veterans Day, the day honoring men and women who have served in the military, on November 11 (the day of the armistice that ended World War I in 1918, on the 11th hour of the 11th day of the 11th month). In the United States, Thanksgiving has always commemorated the Pilgrims' survival of their first winter. It is observed on the fourth Thursday of November. Even in the West and South, where the season bears no resemblance to the late-autumn woods of New England, festive gatherings and tables laden with traditional foods such as turkey, cranberry sauce, and yams or sweet potatoes, mark the common heritage.

Thanksgiving Celebrations Have Left the Farm

While Thanksgiving is certainly one of North America's most anticipated holidays of the year, it is essential to point out that even in rural areas around the United States today, only around one in 10 adults actually works on a farm. Large agribusiness now accounts for much of the farm work, and advances in technology and machination of farm tasks have lessened the labor involved with maintaining crops. Canadians have applied intensive industrial practices to raising their food supply as much as their southern neighbors. North Americans still celebrate the harvest, but the celebration for most, unlike people in many other regions of the world, focuses on the historical aspects of the day and traditional foods eaten, and is not about a direct connection to the land.

Thanksgiving Day Traditions
The Thanksgiving Meal

Thanksgiving for most North Americans is highlighted by an enormous mid- to late-afternoon meal. While it may or may not have been part of the original Thanksgiving feasts, the most widely recognized food eaten on Thanksgiving is turkey. In homes across North America, the turkey is glazed and then roasted for several hours, the smells wafting through homes whether in hot and humid Miami, Florida, or snowy Anchorage,

A guide in colonial costume in Plymouth, Massachusetts describes life for the English Pilgrims and local Native Americans in Plymouth, site of a harvest feast in 1621 that has come to be known as Thanksgiving.

Alaska. Adults spend hours preparing other dishes as the turkey (or in some homes, ham or meatless "turkey") cooks. These dishes are in part made with the foods from North America that were cultivated when the early colonists first landed on the eastern shores. They consist of cranberry sauce, sweet potato dishes, mashed potatoes, breads (which were not part of the first feast, as it would take many tries for the colonists to successfully grow wheat), and pumpkin pie. Other foods associated with Thanksgiving today include pecan pie, stuffing, dressing, and a variety of corn dishes.

Giving Thanks in Church

For Christians in North America, giving thanks at church on the Sunday before and after Thanksgiving is also often part of the harvest observation. In honor of old-world traditions, churches are sometimes decorated with pumpkins, cornucopias, cornstalks, hay bales, Indian corn, fall leaves, wheat, and fall flowers, such as chrysanthemums. Around the

Different Turkey Techniques

According to the National Turkey Federation, 95 percent of people in the United States eat turkey for Thanksgiving. In Hawaii, instead of the traditional butter basting, coffee is sometimes rubbed on the turkey before cooking. In the South, the turkey might be deep fried.

church or Sunday school classrooms, children's pictures of turkey often hang. During Sunday service, congregations sing songs of thanks to God. Often members of congregations, especially in areas where there are high levels of poverty, set up food banks or provide Thanksgiving dinners to those less fortunate.

Unique Customs and Traditions in the United States

Over the years, new customs and practices have been added to Thanksgiving celebrations in the United States. Since the start of the tradition in 1924, in many households on Thanksgiving morning televisions are tuned to the Macy's Thanksgiving Day Parade held in New York City each year. The spectacle includes enormous 40-foot high floats and super-sized helium balloons in the shape

A supervisor at the Salvation Army in St. Louis brings out a turkey for carving during a free Thanksgiving meal for the needy.

Elementary school students perform in the play, "A Native American Welcome." The play is about the first meeting between the Pilgrims and Native Americans at Thanksgiving.

of children's favorite cartoon and movie characters. The last balloon of the parade is always the Santa Claus float. Today approximately 2.5 million people line the streets of Manhattan in New York City, to watch the two and a half mile annual march, and another 44 million viewers around the United States watch from the comfort of their homes. After the parade is over, the television often stays on so that sports fans everywhere can enjoy the numerous Thanksgiving Day football games. Beginning nearly a century ago in 1920, football and "turkey day" have gone hand in hand.

For some in the United States, Thanksgiving is a little more active. Around the country, towns, cities, athletic organizations, and other groups sponsor Turkey Trots, or races of different lengths, in which the community is encouraged to participate. These include special kids' races. Runs might take place on Thanksgiving Day or a day or two before, and

Plymouth Colony, 1621

In many kindergarten classrooms around the United States just before Thanksgiving vacation, children dress up as miniature Pilgrims in buckled black hats and as American Indians with feathered headdress to perform the "first" Thanksgiving meal. They reenact when the English colonists (now called Pilgrims) of Plymouth and the Wampanoag Indians shared a harvest feast in 1621.

One Lucky Turkey

One peculiar Thanksgiving tradition is the annual Thanksgiving Turkey Presentation at the White House Rose Garden in Washington D.C. Since the late 1940s, a few days before Thanksgiving, the president of the United States officially pardons a Thanksgiving turkey, sparing one bird from ending up as the centerpiece of the traditional feast. After this official pardon, the lucky turkey is sometimes flown first class to a destination such as Disneyland in California or Disney World in Orlando, Florida, where it becomes head bird for a Disney Thanksgiving Day Parade.

often a willing adult wears a turkey outfit and runs with the crowd. Other Turkey Trot activities include Thanksgiving costume contests and free pumpkin pies to the race finishers. Proceeds from the race entry fees are frequently donated to local charities and nonprofit organizations in the communities.

Ancient Harvest Festivals from Afar Find a Home in North America

Kwanzaa

A harvest festival called Kwanzaa is celebrated by African Americans in North America who feel strongly about maintaining a connection to their African roots. In 1966, a black studies professor from California named Maulana Karenga created the North American holiday in order to affirm the social and family values of African Americans. The celebration lasts for a week right after Christmas and involves different principles that each family focuses on each day of the week during a candle-lighting ceremony. The celebration concludes on the last day with a community feast. Like Sukkot and Thanksgiving, many Kwanzaa rites are family-centered and revolve around a central feast. This meal, called *Kamaru*, often features traditional African foods such as okra, ground corn, or rice seasoned with cardamom.

Sukkot

Early Jewish settlers to North America brought with them their Sukkot celebrations. Today millions of Jews living in Canada and the United States continue the tradition of constructing a family sukkah and eating their meals in them. In areas where there are large Jewish communities, these sukkahs transform neighborhood yards and decks for several days in the early fall.

Ancient Corn Harvest Festivals Remain Strong through Time and Place

While the relationship between Thanksgiving and the actual first fruits harvest is mostly symbolic in North America today, this is not the case

High school students from Temple Beth-El in Richmond, Virginia, decorate the synagogue's sukkah. A sukkah, or temporary dwelling, is made to celebrate Sukkot, the weeklong Jewish harvest holiday.

One of the more than 3,000 Native American drummers, dancers, and entertainers participate in the annual four-day Festival of Green Corn and Dance in Hartford, Connecticut.

for many American Indian harvest festivals. The Green Corn Festival, or Busk, is widely celebrated by southeastern American Indian tribes, including the Creek, Natchez, Cherokee, and Seminole, every year as the corn is ready to be picked. This can take place anywhere from May to October depending on the region. These celebrations began thousands of years ago and continue on today, even though many tribes were forcibly resettled off their traditional lands during the 18th and 19th centuries to other regions (for example, the Creek were forced out of Georgia and mostly now live in Alabama, Oklahoma, and parts of Florida). Along with the changing dates, the length of the Green Corn Festivals also varies from region to region and tribe to tribe depending on when the corn is ready to be harvested and the specific rites and customs associated with each group. However all Busk observances hold in common the emphasis on renewal of life and of the land and the purification of the self and the community.

Busk Harvest and New Year

Because bringing in a bountiful corn harvest was a matter of life and death for ancient tribes, Busk is often considered a New Year's celebration as well. It is a time where most crimes or bad actions are forgiven (with the exception of serious crimes such as murder) and all are welcome to take part. As is done for many harvest and New Year's festival preparations, the women and children of many southeastern tribes spend the

Little Fire for Big Sun

Some southeastern tribes, such as the Natchez, worshipped the Sun. Like most tribes in this region, their homes were built in uniform rows around a central plaza. For the Natchez, in the middle of the plaza was a temple in which a fire always burned. However, this fire was allowed to die out on the eve of the Green Corn Festival, to be lit again early the next morning, on the festival day. This tradition is still practiced today.

days leading up to the festival intensively cleaning their households, and discarding old clothing and stored food. Inside Creek homes, a household fire traditionally burns continuously from one Busk celebration to the next. Just before the new corn harvest is celebrated, this hearth fire is put out and will stay out until it is lit again during Busk. During these preparations, while the women and children focus on the dwellings, the Creek men are busy sprucing up the ceremonial grounds. They must bring together four new logs to serve as the foundation of the ceremonial fire. When the fire is lit during the festival, each family takes a coal from the ritual fire and relights the fire at home, symbolizing the fresh start of a new year and the successful completion of another harvest.

Purification with the Black Drink

A central purification rite for Busk is the consuming of the Black Drink, a drink made from Yaupon holly leaves that are roasted and brewed to make the liquid. Drinking the Black Drink is believed to help strengthen friendships and communication among the living as well as between the living and the spirits. Yaupon holly contains caffeine and can have the same effects as a laxative on the system. It also causes sweating. Many tribes believe this sweating removes physical and spiritual impurities. The use of this holly among the indigenous tribes of the southeastern United States is widespread. During Busk, the purification rites are followed by the tasting of the first corn of the season, and days of singing, dancing, and eating. Prayer is also important as the tribes give thanks to the Sun, rain, and corn gods. Feasts, dancing, singing, and stickball games traditional to many tribes of this region alternate with times of deep prayer and ritual baths during this intense harvest festival.

Glossary

agribusiness   The integrated production, processing, storage, and distribution of farm equipment and supplies

ancestor worship   Since ancient times, cultures have believed that there is life after death in some form. Communities provided food offerings to their deceased relatives and performed religious rites to keep their spirits pleased. In many parts of the world today, especially Africa, Asia, and Oceana, many still believe the dead have needs to be taken care of by the living and that there is a connection between the dead and the fertility of the land. To honor the connection rites are performed, especially during times of harvest and the festival associated with them.

animism   The belief that plants, trees and other things in nature (the sky, mountains, and rocks) have spirits or souls.

Antarctic Circle   The parallel of latitude that is distant 23"27' from the South Pole. It marks the southern frigid zone.

aqueduct   A channel for moving water from a higher level to a lower level. Aqueducts are often used to move water over long distances.

Arctic Circle   The parallel of latitude 66"33' north, which surrounds the North Pole. Within this area there is at least one day during the year on which the Sun never rises, and one day during the year on which it never sets.

bloodletting   A ritual removal of blood from the body, usually done by making small cuts. Common in ancient times, it is no longer used today except to treat some rare medical conditions.

cash crop   A crop grown to be sold.

colonize   To travel to and settle in a foreign land that has already been settled by groups of people. To colonize can mean to take control of the indigenous groups already in the area or to wield power over them in order to control their human and physical resources.

conquistadores   The 16th-century conquistadores century Spanish conquerors of Mexico, Central America, and Peru.

Coptic Christians   Christian Egyptians who belong to the Coptic Orthodox Church.

cornucopia   A decoration used during harvest holidays that is shaped like a horn and filled with fruit and grain. This decoration originated in Greek times as a curved goat's horn that was a symbol for abundance. It is also known as the "horn of plenty."

depression   When a country or region is affected by lack of jobs, loss of productivity, and an increase in poverty, it is considered to be suffering a severe economic slump known as a depression.

diaspora   The scattering of a people from their homeland. Capitalized, it refers to the Jews of antiquity.

eclipse   When a planet or other astronomical body such as the Sun is blocked from view because a different object (such as the Moon) comes between the observer and the body.

elixir   A beverage made with special ingredients to have curative powers for the drinker

equator   The imaginary line that extends around the Earth and that divides it into two halves. Each half is equal in distance from the North and South Poles. The equator goes through the northern part of South America and Central Africa.

exodus   A mass departure or evacuation from a region or country.

export   A product, such as food crops or manufactured objects, that originates in one country but is shipped out, or exported, to another country for sale and use.

famine   An extreme scarcity of food that leads a region or country's people to experience tremendous hunger or starvation.

Fertile Crescent   The area in the Middle East where the first agricultural societies were born. Because wild wheat and barley grew well in this fertile area, nomadic hunters and animal herders eventually settled down along the lush riverbanks. Towns and civilizations began to take root. It is referred to as a crescent because it is a curved area that extends from south of Jerusalem north along the Mediterranean coast to Syria and east through Iraq then south along the Tigris and Euphrates rivers to the Persian Gulf.

High Holy Days   These are the days celebrated by Jewish people everywhere that begin right after the Jewish New Year, Rosh Hashanah, and end 10 days later with Yom Kippur, the Jewish Day of Atonement. They take place in the seventh month of the Jewish calendar called Tishri. Tishri usually corresponds to September or October on the Gregorian calendar. Rosh Hashanah and Yom Kippur are the most important religious Jewish holidays as well as the most solemn. It is a time when Jews everywhere reflect on the past year and ask for forgiveness for their sins.

Inuit   A term used to designate people indigenous to the Arctic regions of Canada, the United States, Greenland, and Russia.

Islam   The religion of Muslims throughout the world. This religion is based on the word of God that was revealed to the Muslim prophet Muhammad during the seventh century c.e. Islam also refers collectively to the people, culture, and countries where Muslims live.

Israelite   Someone who was part of the ancient group of Hebrew people that originally descended from Jacob, a biblical ancestor of the 12 disciples of Israel.

Jesuit   A person associated with the Society of Jesus, a Roman Catholic group that does missionary and educational work around the world. The Jesuit religious order began in the 16th century with the purpose of defending Catholicism against the Reformation (a movement that wanted to reform some parts of Catholicism and eventually led to the growth of Protestantism).

kosher   Food that has been prepared in a way that is appropriate under Jewish law according to the Torah and other Jewish Holy Books. The Orthodox branches of Judaism will usually only eat food that is kosher. For example, the Torah states that only fish that have fins and scales are kosher (all shellfish are off limits) and also places off limits 24 different species of fowl.

latitude   The distance of a place on the Earth's surface measured from the equator in increments known as degrees, minutes, and seconds.

maypoles   The pole that is put up for May Day celebrations and in pagan times was a symbol of fertility. Today, the maypole is often decorated with flowers and colored ribbons. People dance and sing around the maypole holding onto the ribbons, which become intertwined in colorful patterns.

medieval   A time period known as the Middle Ages in Europe that begins with the fall of the Roman Empire in the 4th and 5th centuries C.E. and ends with the Renaissance of the 14th century. During this time Roman Catholic Christian religious thought took root and religious institutions determined the development of society.

missionary   A religious person who is sent by a religious order to a different region or country to try to spread a particular faith or religion by converting the people who live there. Some missionaries also do social work or provide other aid as part of their mission.

monotheism   The belief in the supremacy of one god (and not many) that began with Judaism more than 4,000 years ago and also includes the major religions of Islam and Christianity.

monsoons   A period of extremely heavy rains, usually in the summer. Often monsoons refer to heavy rains in South Asia

Muslim   Someone who practices the religion of Islam.

New World   A term used to describe the Americas from the point of view of the Western Europeans (especially those from France, England, Portugal, and Spain) who colonized and settled what is today North and South America.

Observant Jew   A Jewish person who practices Judaism, the religion of the Jews. Observant Jews can be part of the Reform, Traditional, or Orthodox communities and not all observant Jews follow all of the Jewish traditions as would Orthodox Jews. However, observant Jews take part in, or observe, the major traditions, holy days, and religious services associated with Judaism.

Orthodox Jew   A Jewish person who strictly follows Jewish laws as set forth by the Holy Books, especially the Torah and the Oral Law that was interpreted in medieval times. For Orthodox Jews, every part of life is directed by their faith, including prayer, how to dress, food and food preparation, relationships between family members, social behavior and customs, and the Sabbath, as well as all holidays.

pagan   The original definition of *pagan* is someone in ancient Europe who lived in the countryside. Over time it has acquired a broader definition and refers to a person or group that does not believe in one god, but often believes in many gods that are closely connected to nature and the natural world.

patron saint   A pious person who has died and is believed to mediate with God for a community or a group of people. This saint often had some kind of historical relationship with the community or place (such as a church). Archers, actors, air travelers, and even accountants have patron saints. Some countries have patron saints.

pilgrimage   A journey undertaken to a specific destination, often for religious purposes

pious   Very religious or devout

pre-Columbian   Of or relating to the period before Christopher Columbus arrived in the Americas

Reform Jew   A Jewish person who believes in a more modern view of Judaism and has embraced changes in some Jewish traditions, such as allowing men and women to sit together in the synagogue or not following the kosher traditions for food preparation. Reform Judaism started in the Diaspora and today a majority of Jews in the United States practice Reform Judaism.

savanna   A level grass plain that is found in tropical and subtropical regions around the world.

shaman   A spiritual guide who a community believes has unique powers to tell the future and to heal the sick. Shamans can mediate or cooperate with spirits for a community's advantage. Cultures that practice shamanism are found all over the world still today.

solstice   The longest or shortest day of the year when the Sun is farthest or closest to the equator. These days occur close to June 21 and December 21 every year. The summer solstice marks the longest day of the year and many harvest festivals take place on or close to this day.

subsistence farming   Farming, or a system of farming, that provides all or almost all of the food needed by the farm family without much left over to sell.

terrace farming   A type of farming done by cutting multiple levels into the sides of a hill so that crops can grow in areas of steep elevation

tuber   An underground stem, such as a potato, that is shortened, thickened, and fleshy, and with buds that may become new plants.

venerate   To view someone with deep respect or to hold someone or something in the highest regard.

yield   The amount of a crop or other creation produced through labor or farming

Bibliography

Amamoo, J. G. *The New Ghana: The Birth of a Nation*. Lincoln, Neb.: Author's Press Choice, 2000.

Cardin, Nina Beth. *The Tapestry of Jewish Time: A Spiritual Guide to Holidays and Life-Cycle Events*. Springfield, N.J.: Behrman House, Inc., 2000

Cohen, Hennig, and Tristram Potter Coffin, eds. *The Folklore of American Holidays*. Detroit, Mich.: Gale Research Co., 1987.

Deetz, James, and Jay Anderson. *Partakers of Plenty: A Study of the First Thanksgiving*. Plymouth, Mass.: Plymouth Plantation, 1972.

Jackson, Ellen. *The Autumn Equinox: Celebrating the Harvest*. Minneapolis, Minn.: Millbrook Press, 2003.

Mazzeo, Donatello, and Chiara Silvi Antonini. *Ancient Cambodia*. New York: Grosset & Dunlap, 1978.

Minnick-Taylor, Kathleen. *Kwanzaa: How to Celebrate It in Your Home*. Madison, Wisc.: Praxis Publications, 1994.

Further Resources

Books

1621, A New Look at Thanksgiving. By Catherine O'Neill Grace and Sisse Brimberg. Published in 2001 by National Geographic Children's Books, Washington, D.C. Accompanied by gorgeous photographs this book looks at Thanksgiving from the point of view of the Wampanoag Indians.

African and Caribbean Celebrations. By Gail Johnson. Published in 2007 by Hawthorn, Stroud, UK. An introduction to the festivals of Africa and the African diaspora in the Caribbean. Covering Junkonnu, Carnival, and the harvest festival Crop Over, this illustrated book also includes stories, games, songs, and craft activities that are associated with these celebrations.

America's Parade: A Celebration of Macy's Thanksgiving Day Parade. Published in 2001 by Time, Inc., New York. *Life* magazine's history of the most famous Thanksgiving Day parade in the United States with spectacular photographs.

China. By Hugh Sebag-Montefiore. Published in 2007 by DK Children, New York. A photograph-based exploration of Chinese culture and traditions, as well food, animals, government, nature, and family information. The 72-page book comes with a Clip Art CD that might be useful for classroom projects.

Earth Prayers From around the World: 365 Prayers, Poems, and Invocations for Honoring the Earth. Edited by Elizabeth Roberts and Elias Amidon. Published in 1991 by HarperSanFrancisco. Inuit songs; Bible verses; Mayan, Hindu, and Egyptian prayers; contemporary poetry; and Zuni chants are just a few examples of the range of entries in this book, all emphasizing the importance of the Earth and its bounty for all cultures in all corners of the world.

Enduring Harvests: Native American Foods and Festivals for Every Season. By E. Barry Kavisch. Published in 2001 by Author's Choice Press, New York. This book, is both a guide to Native American foods and an introduction to more than 70 festivals where these foods are traditionally served. The book is divided by seasons and begins with harvest festivals.

Hinduism. By Ranchor Prime. Published in 2005 by Firefly Books, Scarborough, Ontario, Canada. A colorful reference book for young adults that provides clear information about a complex religious belief system.

Midsummer: Magical Celebrations of the Summer Solstice. By Anna Franklin. Published in 2002 by Llewellyn Publications, Woodbury, Minn. This book contains pretty much everything to know about the origins and modern practices of Midsummer festivals as well as how to create one of your own. While not a book designed with young adults in mind, the information on the lore and history is useful for a deeper study of this important harvest festival.

Mooncakes and Hungry Ghosts: Festivals of China. By Carol Stepanchuk and Charles Wong. Published in 1991 by China Books & Periodicals, Inc., San Francisco. An overview of the festivals of China broken down by Festivals of the Living, Dead, Earth, Water, Wind, and Fire, as well as Festivals of Romance and Compassion, and Survival and Marriage. Included is the Mid-Autumn Harvest Moon Festival.

Thanksgiving Day in Canada. By Krys Val Lewicki. Published in 2005 by Napoleon Publishing, Toronto. A book about the Toronto origins of Canada's Thanksgiving celebration that includes many colorful illustrations and an original Canadian Thanksgiving song.

The Encyclopedia of World Religions. By Robert Ellwood and Gregory Alles, Eds. Published in 2007 by Facts On File, New York. A comprehensive encyclopedia of religious terms and religions, including ancient and indigenous religions, major world religions, and new religions.

Web Sites

Biodiversity International. http://news.bioversityinternational.org/index.php?itemid=697. This site provides an interesting article focusing on the Dagomba society of northern Ghana entitled the "The Cultural Role of Yams."

Harvest Festivals.Net. http://www.harvestfestivals.net/harvestfestivals.htm. A Web site with information on more than 40 harvest festivals celebrated world-wide. While the entries are quite short this site provides a good starting point for research on specific festivals.

The Jewish Virtual Library. http://www.jewishvirtuallibrary.org/jsource/Judaism/holiday5.html. This online encyclopedia provides extensive and easy-to-follow explanations of virtually every aspect of Judaism. Here, one can better understand Sukkot and all Jewish celebrations, as well as the history of Judaism, important Jewish women, the Holocaust, biographies of famous Jews in every field imaginable, and vital information on Israel.

Picture Credits

Index

⁶ℛₒ

Page numbers in *italic* indicate illustrations.

About the Author

Ann Morrill is a freelance writer, occasional bilingual editor, and adjunct college Spanish instructor living in Colorado. Her published writing includes poetry, opinion pieces, Spanish language phonics books, conservation articles, and uncategorizable creative nonfiction. She holds a master's degree in Latin American studies from the University of New Mexico and a BA in history from Carleton College. When not writing or teaching, she enjoys hiking, reading, drinking coffee, and hanging out with her husband and two boys, Lucas and Marcos.